DEFINING MOMENTS
S.O.S

Stories of Survival

Real People Solving Real Problem

MELANIE WARNER | AMBER TORRES

Copyright © 2020 Defining Moments Press, Inc.

All rights reserved. No part of this book may be reproduced in any form without permission in writing from the author. Reviewers may quote brief passages in reviews.

DISCLAIMER No part of this publication may be reproduced or transmitted in any form or by any means, mechanical or electronic, including photocopying or recording, or by any information storage and retrieval system, or transmitted by email without permission in writing from the author. Neither the author nor the publisher assumes any responsibility for errors, omissions, or contrary interpretations of the subject matter herein.

Any perceived slight of any individual or organization is purely unintentional. Brand and product names are trademarks or registered trademarks of their respective owners.

Defining Moments™ is a registered Trademark

Editing: Amber Torres
Cover Design: Defining Moments Press, Inc
Author's Photo Courtesy of: Lance Pearce

Contents

DEDICATION vi

INTRODUCTION vii

CHAPTER 1: TURNING YOUR MESS INTO YOUR MESSAGE 11
    The End Was the Beginning By Melanie Warner 11
    Kidnapped at 14 By Amber Torres 16
    Daughter of Deep Darkness By Tara Murney 24
    Courage to Grow By Shiran Cohen 30
    When the Only Way Out is Through By Karen Loenser 36
    Making Health and Happiness a #1 Priority By Keri Faith Knudtson 42

CHAPTER 2: ULTIMATE SURVIVAL 50
    It is Easy for Me to Take the Next Step By Heidi Nye 50
    The Reality of Life With an Eating Disorder By Devyn Faz 56
    A Bad Pitch By Bob Shield 62
    Fantasy is Full of Adventure By Toni Barnett 67
    The Power of Prayer By Denard Fobbs 73
    In Case Tomorrow Never Comes By CaSandra Smith 77

CHAPTER 3: TURNING YOUR VICE INTO YOUR VICTORY 83
    In Memory of Amy Wall By Joe Avila 83
    Don't Hide the Scars By Flindt Andersen 90

Freedom in Forgiveness By Toni Odonnell 93
My Own Teen Challenge By Charlie Campbell 98
Portraits of Hope By Lance Pearce 102
A Near Fatal Decision By Michael Edgar 105

CHAPTER 4: FAMILY MATTERS 109
One Decision that Changed My Family Forever By Clara Hinton 109
Surviving to Thriving By Alicia Anne 114
The Trauma After the Trauma By Ann Justi 119
An Oscar Worthy Performance By Shannon P. Murree 124
I Never Knew You Were in There By Alicia Dias 131
The Road to Nowhere By Diana Houk 137

CHAPTER 5: DEFYING THE ODDS 142
Spoonful of Sugar By Mike Riddle 142
The Blind Blogger By Maxwell Ivey 146
Out of the Darkness, Retrieving Your Power From Your Past
By Mara Momsen 153
Finding My Summit By Kimberly Leslie 159

CHAPTER 6: HOPE AFTER LOSS 166
Down the Rabbit's Hole By Mary Ellen Wasielewski 166
Perceive to Achieve By Neal Hooper 172
Dark Effect of Suicide By Hannah Brown 176
Dying to Live By Linda Espinoza 179

CHAPTER 7: DARING ESCAPES 185
I Survived Human Trafficking By Debra Rush 185
Lost By John Warner 190

My American Dream By Eli Sotelo 193

Captain of My Own Ship By William Lurcott 200

Animal Karma By Eric Stanosheck 205

Chowchilla Children: Kidnapped, Buried Alive and Survived...
By Lynda Carrejo Labendeira 210

Fleeing Iran For Freedom By Soodabeh Mokry, RN, CHt 219

CONCLUSION 229

ACKNOWLEDGEMENTS 232

ABOUT THE AUTHORS 233

ABOUT DEFINING MOMENTS PRESS 235

OTHER #1 BEST SELLING BOOKS
BY DEFINING MOMENTS™ PRESS 237

Dedication

To Heidi Nye, who passed away a few days before our book was released. We are so honored to share your light with the world. We will continue to share your story to inspire others who are fighting for their lives every day.

This book is dedicated to my son, Carson Warner Kennedy, who taught me how to be a survivor. To my kids, Kyla, Cole & Hudson – who taught me why I need to be a survivor. To my parents, John and Judy Warner, who taught me what I need to survive anything - is faith.

— Melanie Warner

This book is dedicated to my children, Gabe and Vicky, who gave me the most meaningful title that I have ever known - Mother. I love you both with all my heart.

To my Pastor, Lisa Satterberg, for praying for me daily, nurturing my spiritual walk, showing me what it means to be a woman of God and always pointing me to the Word of God. Your investment in me helped to birth this book.

To Heidi Nye for graciously sharing your story and inspiring those around you to always "take the next step". We are thankful that this book is part of your legacy on earth and honored to share your mighty story. In case I didn't say it often enough, your story is going to help so many people.

— Amber Torres

Introduction

Death is a hard thing to accept. But how do you deal with the death of everything around you, yet you are still alive?

At one point - my son, my marriage and my business were ALL on life support. My son died in my arms from a medical error. A week later - my business advisors told me to shut down my company, that I was losing too much money. Then a therapist told me that I needed to end my marriage, that things would never change and by staying, it was compromising the safety of my kids.

Not only did I lose my son, but then I lost my marriage of 16 years, my business of 20 years, all my money, my homes, the dream of my perfect family, my career. At 41 years old, I was a single mom with three kids – starting over.

I had given everything to everyone else, financially supported my family for sixteen years, volunteered at inner city schools, donated blood, donated so much to so many, paid all the bills, cooked all the meals, did all the dishes, kissed every boo boo, dropped what I was doing to help anyone and everyone - and now I was the one heading towards welfare, being audited by the IRS for years and facing certain bankruptcy of my life and dreams?

It was so unimaginable to feel like I was living the American dream one minute with millions of dollars, money in savings, good credit, affirmation of success, kids doing well in school, a loving husband, a beautiful six bedroom house with a huge backyard, a pool, two BMW's, respect and admiration from my community, my health, my kids' health, a great family, assets, stocks, a rental property, great friends – and then to such an extreme and overwhelming loss of everything I knew. I went from hero to zero - overnight! From Prada to nada... in an instant.

I had never been a depressed person, no matter what my challenges were in life. I was always positive and always believed in justice, love, the bright side, God is good, work hard and you will be rewarded, live your life as a good person and good things will come to you, be kind to others, be generous, give from your heart and it will come back to you, etc. Now every single thing I thought was true was being compromised, challenged, denied, or even just ignored.

I prayed and prayed until my hands were raw and lost over thirty pounds in tears alone – yet I got silence. No answers, no divine wisdom, no booming "I'm sorry for your troubles". Why was God punishing me? Why did my life have to fall apart so badly? What was the lesson I obviously so desperately needed?

I often asked, "what would Jesus do?" And I often thought about how Jesus might handle things today. He had never been married. He had never had kids. He had never been a woman... in labor...giving birth. He never had PMS. He never had to drive a car.....in Los Angeles.....during rush hour. He never had to discipline a child or get them to three different schools on time - all at the same time.

Jesus had never been a single parent, divorced, or a business owner, or had to collect money from people who owed it and didn't pay it. He was the only man in flesh who never sinned, he was the perfect man – who never got married! He was kind, gentle, patient, loving, forgiving – and they CRUCIFIED him. So, how in the world did he ever turn that message into such a popular life model? Be nice and the world will screw you over – but be nice anyways? That's like saying "give all your money to those less fortunate and then go broke". I'm sure there would be people lining up for that. Oh, wait. I did that, too.

Sure, there were times where I questioned God – but never, ever blamed him or turned my back on him. Often when we are in despair, it means we have turned our backs on God. If we truly had faith and knew that he was in control of our lives, then we would have the peace to know that it's OK if we don't know what's around the corner – but either way we are not alone. Faith is knowing inherently that everything will be ok. That all the things you struggle with are designed to give you what you ask for.

If you pray for wisdom, then the only way you get it is from your experiences. The worse the experience, the deeper the lesson, the greater the wisdom. It has to be a whole body experience so that you feel it so deep – you know in your bones what to do next time. If you pray for peace, then sometimes you have to survive a war in order to have peace. The war is often inside of us.

I learned that God did not abandon me. I abandoned myself. God was not simply allowing horrible things to happen in my life. My bad choices, my own free will got me into this mess and He was still willing to pull me out of it – even after my own stupid self got me in the mess. God was not punishing me. He was protecting me. I was not being buried, I was being planted - for something so much bigger that I could not see then.

All the things that crumbled in my life did so because they were never built on a solid foundation. You can't build a business on a tightrope and expect it to survive. You can't build a marriage on quicksand and expect it to be stable. You can't make a big mess and then blame God for it – but He will be there to help you clean it up, to pick up the pieces and help you see the big picture of your life.

Maybe you don't like the picture? Then change the damn channel. You have the remote to your own life so stop blaming other people if you don't like what you see. It's easy to live in denial, checked out and pretending that we actually love soap operas. But when you are living in one – it's not as exciting to watch the ups and downs. Roller coasters are fun, thrilling, and exciting – but they are designed to only last a few minutes for a reason. When you are on that loop de loop every day, it only makes you nauseous.

For me, it had started five years earlier and I had felt that daily conflict and struggle. It was like the movie "Groundhog Day" and I was living in my

DEFINING MOMENTS SOS (Stories of Survival)

own personal hell and experiencing the same day all over again and again and again.

This book is about falling... and falling hard. But, more importantly, it's about how to get back up. No matter what you are facing, there is someone else who has already survived it. The key is to connect with others who understand so that you never have to walk that journey alone.

This book is about my story - and so many others who survived their own "Defining Moment". As you read it, remember that it is an interactive experience. We have tools to help you through any hardship - emotional, physical, financial or relationships.

To stay connected, or for additional support, please email me directly at: Melanie@MyDefiningMoments.com. We can even set up a brief call to see what resources you need the most and where we can best offer support for any circumstance.

Sending you love, light & positive juju.

Melanie Warner

1

Turning Your Mess into Your Message

The End Was the Beginning

By Melanie Warner

I remember a day in February 2011 because it finally felt like the end. And if it was truly the end, then at least I would stop falling and hit the bottom. If I could just reach the bottom, then I could start over – but the worst thing was falling and falling and falling – while still trying to be Pollyanna.

It felt like I fell off a tall building and as I fell past each floor I would say, "I'm ok so far." At least when you hit the bottom, even if you break in a million pieces – then you can see the pieces that need to be picked up. You have the pieces to put your story back together or at least start over.

When you are still in the process of falling – that horrible, desperate feeling is always there. Often, the anticipation of impending doom or loss is far worse than the actual loss. You wake up every day, knowing there is a dark cloud over your life before you even get out of bed. Living in it, fighting it, feeling it, processing it, accepting it and finally surrendering to it – was such a long process.

I Felt So Trapped!

When I filed personal bankruptcy, it put the divorce on hold. We couldn't finalize anything financial in the divorce until the bk was final. If I didn't file it, I would have lost my house to foreclosure. The only reason I filed personal is because I shut down a business and it had personal guarantees. So, if I didn't file, I would have lost my house. If I did file, then I risked losing my business and all my income.

I was also being accused of owing $2 million in taxes to the IRS. They tacked on an 80% penalty, so it was more like $3.6 million, I really thought my life was over, or that I would be working the rest of my life to pay this off or defend myself.

Losing My Dream Home

When I actually let go and sobbed, my cries seemed even louder and lonelier as they echoed in this large, empty, cavernous, quiet home when the kids are gone, and I was all alone. When I took off the mommy mask for a brief moment to grieve my losses... before someone else needed something or another looming threat popped up. I was an emotional mess.

Regrowth

Think of a once beautiful tree, stripped of its beauty, pruned, cut, disfigured, bare, but through the dark, seemingly dead, branches flow silently and secretly, the life-giving sap. As the tree bends in the wind, even carries the frost of winter in a beautiful and elegant way that others can see... patiently waiting until the sun of Spring comes new life, leaves, bud, blossom, fruit. And the fruit is a thousand times better after pruning. You are in the hands of a Master Gardener. Spring is always close. Just like the tree, you can bear the winter knowing there is always a Spring. The sun is always sending you love and strength, even above the gray clouds.

The Race

It is not the start of the race that hurts, nor the pace, nor the long stretch. It's when the goal is in sight, that the heart and nerves and courage and muscles are strained almost beyond human endurance, almost to the breaking point. If you run well, even hard and brave, but give up just before the goal, with victory just beyond a few more steps - then it means your courage failed. Only YOU decide when to give up or when to keep pushing. The spectators are always cheering and always encouraging you the entire way, especially for that one last sprint to victory. Keep running and don't ever look back.

Feeling Loved

If you are suffering from a broken heart, then you are not alone. You are loved beyond measure and don't need a piece of chocolate, a rose, a hug, or even a whisper from anyone to know that.

If you are feeling sad or lonely, or your heart is bleeding today...YOU can do something about it. Think of this...You cannot receive love until you love yourself first. What we see in others is a mere reflection of ourselves in other people. You can only accept the love that you feel inside. If you don't love yourself, you will think it is love when someone is abusive, even though you know you should be treated better. If you were treated better, you would lose interest because it would not match the feeling you have inside, so it betrays your belief. We reject anything more than what we feel we truly deserve. When you love and accept yourself, then you will no longer be attracted to people who don't treat you with love, kindness, and respect.

If they only throw you crumbs, it's because YOU are starving yourself. If they dumped you, it's because YOU dumped yourself. If they abuse you, it's because YOU abuse yourself. You will learn that you don't have to live simply to manage expectations or disappointments. The bottom line is if you want people to treat you better start by treating YOURSELF better. Be your own soulmate and do something great for yourself today and every day!

I always thought my children would learn how to love themselves based on how much I love them. Now I understand that they will learn to treat themselves the way I treat myself. The greatest gift you can ever give your children is your own happiness!

The Turning Point

For those of you who are in the pit right now. I can tell you that things WILL be ok. No matter what. All of my failures have led directly to all the success I am having today. Once I learned how to make better choices, rebuild on a solid foundation and focus my time on things that generated income - everything changed. I was able to rebuild my entire life in a short amount of time. Money is not emotional, but the lack of money is. Not having money for basic expenses made everything else much worse. I understood that if I wanted to make positive changes in my life for myself and my family - then making money was a big part of it.

As I mentioned, after my divorce and the 2008 crash, I lost the home of my dreams to foreclosure. Then I went through bankruptcy, tax audits and even tax court. I also went from making $1 million year to living on unemployment when I shut down my only source of income.

I had to meet myself at my means and support three kids on $1,800 month.

It felt like I would never be able to buy another home for the rest of my life.

I even had to represent myself in tax court. That was probably the scariest time of my life, besides losing my son. But I survived it. In fact, they conceded on all charges and were willing to accept an offer and compromise from $3.6 million for a payment of only $5,000! There is always a solution if you trust the truth in the situation.

I didn't know what I could do until I was tested. What I learned from all of these trials has prepared me for the success I am having today.

Since then, I've worked really hard to rebuild my life financially, repair my credit and pay off all of my debt. I am current on all taxes. I raised my credit score 130 points in less than 90 days. Even when I had very little, I never missed one payment... for the last 12 years.

I started working with mentors and listening to the people who had what I wanted. I paid what little money I had to learn from experts on how to save time and money by knowing what they had learned the hard way. I understood that personal growth was the one thing that would make a difference in all aspects of my life - physically, emotionally, financially, spiritually, and mentally.

The most important lesson was that my mindset had really been the biggest catalyst for growth. I learned that I first had to solve the problem in my head before I could solve the problem outside of me. So, the more I worked on myself and repaired the relationship with myself - the better all of my relationships got. The more I focused on finding and creating residual income, the better my finances got.

Transformation Tip

Are you living in a mid-life crisis? Or a mid-life castle? Both are choices that you made from daily thoughts, actions and decisions that led to where you are today. Positive thoughts bring positive energy results. Negative thoughts bring negative energy results. Change your thoughts and it changes everything!

Melanie Warner *is a #1 bestselling author, speaker, publisher, and entrepreneur. She is the founder of the Defining Moments book series that offer positive stories of hope and healing from people who have overcome extreme challenges in life.*

Warner was a successful magazine publisher for over 20 years and then tragedy hit her family when her son died. That emotional shut down led to divorce, shutting down her company, then bankruptcy, foreclosure and even tax court. What had taken her 20 years to build was gone over night. She had to rebuild her entire life from scratch - and found a way to do it in only two years.

This experience inspired her to write the first book of the series - Defining Moments: Coping With the Loss of a Child as a resource for bereaved families. Her book hit the bestseller list in only two weeks.

After that, she was inundated with requests to help others get their book completed, published, and marketed. She teaches people how to write a book that is profitable and how to align it with a business that makes a difference for others.

Melanie is also a book coach who helps people write, publish, and launch their own books. Do you want to share your story with the world? Apply to work with us online at www.MyDefiningMoments.com or email Melanie@MyDefiningMoments.com

---

Kidnapped at 14

By Amber Torres

"There are all these moments you think you won't survive.
And then you survive."

— David Levithan

I grew up in a suburban neighborhood in Clovis, California. I lived with my two parents and younger sister. I enjoyed school, playing soccer, gymnastics and doing crazy flips on the trampoline. I had a dog named Curly Sue (I was a 90's kid).

By the age of seven, I can recall my relationship with my mother being strained. I felt emotionally abandoned by her. I recall telling her "I love you" and her seeming uncomfortable and never saying it back. In times when my feelings were hurt, they were often invalidated. In interactions with my mother, an apology was something I never received, and hugs were extremely rare.

My father routinely came to her defense at the time and well into adulthood saying, "That's just how your mother is." I now recognize that she grew up in a different time and her love language was different than mine. That coupled with the fact that I was independent and strong-willed from the time I was a toddler, made it difficult for her to parent me versus my sister who was more obedient.

By the age of nine there was an unhealthy dynamic in my home. Whatever underlying tension existed between my mom and dad was coming to the surface. There seemed to be an unexplainable divide in our family. My mom and sister vs me and my dad.

Subconsciously I began to take on the error in thinking that I wasn't worthy of love. It was not something I intentionally thought and believed; instead, it was merely that a core relationship in my life showed me that my role was to beg for validation and love.

The summer before high school I met a boy who was "so cute". He didn't make me beg for affection. Instead, he showed me all the attention that I craved. He was charming, and before I knew it, we were in a sexual relationship. He was my first intimate experience and, truth be told, our relationship went from 0 to 100. I didn't regret having sex with him immediately after but, after some time passed, I began to feel increasingly guilty.

I had been raised in the Catholic church and would visit my best friend's Protestant church on occasion so sex before marriage went against my personal convictions. I quickly found myself in a destructive cycle of fornication, guilt, remorse, crossing my fingers hoping I wasn't pregnant then promising myself that, if my period came, I would no longer engage in sexual activity. I never put myself on birth control because I felt like it was solidifying my decision to have sex with this boy. I desperately wanted to stop but felt like cutting off our sexual relationship might result in no relationship at all. I was betraying my heart and body, trading sex for the love that I so desperately needed.

On one occasion, after I had just had a pregnancy scare, I can clearly remember thinking to myself, "That sucks. I would stop (having sex) if my mom loved me" then envisioning being cut off from my source of validation. A boy who would ditch me to be with his friends and only stop by late in the evening when everyone in my house was asleep. I would leave my window unlocked and he would slip inside my room sometimes. Only in adulthood, once God started to show me just how precious and valuable I truly am, would I realize how that routine made an imprint on me.

My relationship with my mother consisted of no relational intimacy but every morning she would sigh and tell me critically that I was wearing too much makeup. Sometimes she would tell me that I looked like a hooker. The boundaries of parent and child were so blurred that I actually thought that I didn't have to listen to her when she told me to take the makeup off.

Her voiced disapproval would set the tone for that day. One time a friend came over and told me jokingly, "Your mom acts like she doesn't like you!" She was right in that you could cut the tension with a knife.

Despite not feeling loved, I was fortunate enough to never fall into the drug and alcohol scene, but I did engage in risky behavior. I was dependent on the approval of my boyfriend and, on one occasion, I snuck out and hitchhiked to his home late at night. I was back early in the morning and no one knew. No problem at all. On the second occasion, I was not so lucky- I returned home the victim of an attempted rape.

Perhaps I got too confident after my first late night rendezvous, but I offered to walk to my boyfriend's house to see him since he was always coming to my home. The foolishness of youth had me convinced that I was invincible. I had only gotten one street away from my parent's house when a truck pulled up beside me. A man asked me if I needed a ride. I told him the cross streets to where I was going and he said he could take me there. My destination was only a short distance. He drove south in the correct direction to the next stop light and then merged into the U-Turn lane to go north. As he pulled into the U-Turn lane he said, "Oh, I'm supposed to go that way huh?" to imply that turning into the U-Turn lane was a mistake.

Alarm bells didn't go off until after he made the "wrong turn" and I answered, "Yeah." Then, he clinched the back of my shirt and told me, "I'm going to take you out to the field and you're gonna have sex with me." I began to panic on the inside but stayed quiet trying to figure out how to escape. I was frozen and in shock. Everything was in slow motion and I felt like I was watching a movie.

At the time, everything north of my parent's house was field and countryside. As we approached the main cross street to my parent's house, I realized that I might not come back alive if he took me out to the field. I started feeling for the door handle, in shock. Even at the time, I knew I was moving really slow and in an obvious manner. I was so numb to what I was experiencing that it was hard for me to gather myself. He told me, "Now honey, don't try to jump out, you're going to hurt yourself."

As I saw the back of my parent's housing complex, I knew I was a goner. I began to pray and begged God to save me. We drove a short while longer and, in a miraculous twist of events, there was a law enforcement truck parked on the west side of the road we were traveling on. I started to swerve the steering wheel and honk the horn loudly like a siren in the night.

Beep!! Beep!! Beep, beep beeeeeeeeeep!!!!

The man had always maintained a calm demeanor even when he had previously told me that he was going to feed me some meat. As I honked the horn, he said in a very rational manner, "Now honey...honey, don't honk the horn..."

"Let me out!!" I screamed.

"Stop honking" he said, trying to convince me to relent.

"Then let me out! Let me out! Let me OUT!!!" I screamed as I continued to turn the wheel to make the car swerve while honking the horn. At one point, as the car was swerving, I kicked the window on my side of the car.

Nothing happened like I thought it would but, luckily, I had already caught the attention of the sheriff. He started following the truck I was in with his lights flashing.

My attacker pulled over to the side of the road and the truck came to a complete stop.

I flung the door open and yelled, "Help me!" as I stuck my head out into the dark night which was illuminated with the flashing lights of several patrol vehicles.

"Get back in the car!!" an officer yelled. I was shocked to see that he was pointing a gun at the truck I was in while using the door of his vehicle as a shield. I couldn't figure out how so many law enforcement vehicles had gotten there so quickly. There were at least three of them!

The sheriff had my attacker exit the vehicle first. As he got out, he said, "She said if I paid her, she would have sex with me." I was very naïve at the time despite having a "serious" boyfriend and I remember being shocked that he would even say that.

He was arrested and I eventually had to go to court. When the officer who was parked on the side of the road took the stand, he said that he wasn't supposed to be on the road he was on that night but decided to take a different route to his destination. Not only was he driving on a road he wasn't planning on taking, he just decided to park in that spot because he had to fill out some paperwork that was left unfinished from earlier that evening. He said he had only been at that spot for a few minutes and was only planning on being there for a few minutes longer when the truck I was in came swerving down the road. His presence was an answer to my prayer.

This incident was a *defining moment* for me because it was the first time in my life that God showed me that I was worth saving and protecting.

After the incident, I started going to counseling to address any trauma resulting from the attack. Surprisingly, I spent more time in counseling talking about my feelings of neglect and sadness over my relationship with my mother than I did about the incident. Over a period of time, my counselor convinced me to share my feelings with my mother. It took everything I had in me, but I did share my feelings and my mother explained that she grew up in a different time and wasn't raised to give hugs.

Things remained the same after this conversation in regard to her expression of love and I made horrible choices until becoming pregnant with my son at 15 from the same boyfriend. Due to my pregnancy, my father didn't want me to be exposed to ruthless questions by my attacker's defense attorney, so we offered a plea bargain which my attacker took-- I believe it was three years of probation with a few additional stipulations.

My counselor and I did talk about the attack though and I worked through my feelings about the incident. The first few months after the attack, I had periodic nightmares. What started off as me being a victim in those nightmares eventually turned into me dominating the dreams, defending myself and being the victor that God created me to be! My counselor said that it is common for the nature of people's dreams to change as they progress in their healing process.

As time passed, I got to a place where I didn't even think about the attack anymore, but I did the work. I would say that I felt *completely* restored after about three years. After about five years, I didn't even think about the incident. It was not repressed but thoroughly worked through.

It's been 23 years since I survived a kidnapping and it honestly is just a part of my past in the same way that my best friend in fifth grade was named Lana; it's just another detail in my life story. I always tell people that you can tell you are truly healed from an incident when there is no shame, no guilt, and no residual fears or triggers. You embrace the lesson, but the pain is no longer raw. You grow from the experience and become better. Wiser.

I was spared in this incident but that doesn't mean that I have not had battles since. The battle of my LIFE was learning how to not just assert my boundaries but follow through with them. My need to maintain core relationships in my life, regardless of the cost, stemmed from a place of brokenness.

When people are used to controlling you, they will hang on to that control with the jaws of life. If you dare to follow through with your boundaries and put up parameters to safeguard yourself and those you are responsible for, you will receive pushback. You might be called selfish. You may be made to feel guilty. People may lie about you and prescribe intent by saying that your motives are not pure. You may be accused of unforgiveness. If kids are involved, you could be accused of using your children as pawns when you are just trying to create healthy parameters around people's contact with them.

Boundaries may sound something like "You can come to my home to visit but my children can't be at your home without me (for the time being until trust is restored or as a general rule) " or "Please do not pick my child up at school without my knowledge and permission." We ought to trust people and give them access to us equal to the level of trust that they have earned.

And there is nothing holy or healthy about maintaining detrimental relationships in order to gain the approval of others. Eventually, the situation escalates to become so unhealthy (and sometimes unsafe), that you can't even justify allowing it. Every relationship should be reciprocal and comprised of mutual respect.

To God be the glory, what I have learned is that you don't have to struggle with people over the authority that belongs to you.

As I write this story, my intent is not to expose anyone. It is to explain the dynamics of my experience as a teenage girl who was looking for love in all the wrong places. As a grown woman, I realize the error in my ways in that I handed over my power as a teenager. I allowed the actions of others to completely determine my actions. I made detrimental choices that went against my personal convictions for the love and approval of others. I was so desperate for love that I would accept the scraps that were given to me.

These days, I have a standard for the close relationships in my life. I genuinely love myself and carefully weigh out the cost of every relationship. I know how to discern when a person doesn't respect me and wants to operate in a way that only serves them. I also know when to show people grace, realizing that they are only human, prone to mistakes like we all are. Every relationship in my life is healthy and intentional.

Perhaps the most beautiful thing that I have learned is how to release pain and unforgiveness. To not hang on to the past. And to not let accusations that my actions are motivated by unforgiveness affect me. When we let go of our negative emotions and truly make peace with our experiences, we are light as a feather.

Transformation Tip

First and foremost, I have to state the obvious-DON'T get in the car with strangers. Even if they know your name. Even if you have conversed with them online. Secondly, if you find yourself going through a trial, PRAY. Prayer works! Once you have prayed, trust that if God doesn't completely deliver you from a situation, he will give you the grace to go through it. Every trial serves a purpose, and nothing happens to us before first passing through the hand of God. Sometimes God allows us to go through a situation so that we can be more like His son-Jesus. Embrace every season and recognize it as an opportunity to gain wisdom.

Amber Torres *earned a BS degree in business management and a certificate in marketing from CSU Fresno in 2011. She currently works in publishing. She is the mother of two children and a volunteer Child Ambassador for World Vision; a Christian Humanitarian organization that works to address the root causes of poverty and injustice (*www.worldvision.org*). World Vision uses the child sponsorship model. As a Child Ambassador, Amber helps to connect children in developing countries with viable sponsors while World Vision works to make advancement in the child's community sustainable.*

To sponsor a child, go to: www.worldvision.org/sponsor-a-child?campaign=320059104

Amber can be reached through email at Amber@mydefiningmoments.com

Daughter of Deep Darkness

By Tara Murney

For a greater part of my life, my most prominent teacher has been depression. I once had 26 journals in my possession- my personal tool kit of self-therapy. My experience with traditional therapy was that it lacked emotional connection and trust. I personally believe the only way any therapist can utterly understand a patient, is to swim in the dark waters that drowned them in the first place. I was simply another victim of abuse, sitting in a chair, sharing a similar story on a clock.

In January 2020, I found myself sitting across from a therapist at a local hospital, explaining how I managed to overcome depression, PTSD, and many attempts at suicide while he was jotting notes. He stated that, out of all the patients he had seen over the years, especially noting the fact that I had scored 10/11 for clinical depression, I was a rarity.

Puzzled, he leaned into me and asked, "How you did you manage all this without medication or therapy?"

I replied, "Easy. I chose to bet on myself, my own rescue, zero compromise."

Resilience is not easy, it requires patience. Much like a flower, it must be cultivated over time. I implemented small shifts every day to work towards a goal of balance, and treating both mind and body as one, which is key to success in achieving a well-balanced life.

On a hot and sunny summer day in 1994, my youth was somewhat frozen in time when a man, fifteen years my senior, scooped me up. I was drugged, trafficked, and later branded much like cattle are. The events of the next two years were so traumatizing for me that I buried them, immersing myself in drugs to numb and forget as much as I could. This man, I'll call him Bob, managed to get into my head and make me so fearful and dependent on him that I would spend two years trauma bonded to him. Through his abuse and exploitation of me, he managed to break me down to the point where I was convinced that he was the only person who could love me.

Our relationship, if you can even call it that, was volatile and dysfunctional. At one point he tried to drown me. On another occasion, he held me on the roof of a car while driving 120 KM/HR and threatened to let me go stating that no one would miss me or even care.

For two years, he maintained a detrimental grip on me. Although I still lived at home with my parents, I would take off and stay with Bob for days at a time without telling anyone where I was. Instead of being in school, I would spend days at his house drugged up and exploited. It's hard for many to understand the complicated nature of a trauma bond and the brainwashing that comes with it. I grew up in a home where my father was angry most of the time, so I became accustomed to an environment of turbulence. My relationship with Bob paralleled my relationship with my own father who seemed to always be angry.

After meeting Bob, my mental health took a turn for the worse. His treatment of me confirmed what I already believed about myself-that I was unworthy and undeserving of love and respect. His exploitation of me stripped me of all dignity. Months after meeting him, I found myself on a bridge along a desolate road at three in the morning ready to take my own life. Cars rarely drove along that road so I knew I wouldn't be interrupted.

As I peered down at the ground, a car pulled up and a man exited the car. He stood in the cold and talked to me for 40 minutes. To this day, I often wonder who that man was that talked a desperate 14-year-old girl off a ledge then sat on a curb next to her telling her that everything was going to be okay. He told me about his life. He reminded me that, even though people can be cruel, there is so much to live for. He placed his hand on mine and gave me a fatherly pep talk. That man saved my life.

Roughly a year later, in early February 1995, my mother was involved in a horrific car accident with my brother which would inevitably change the dynamics of my family for the worst. Besides the physical ailments that she endured, she was soon diagnosed with D.I.D (Dissociative Identity Disorder) and developed 30+ personalities, ranging from a six-year-old little girl up to a death dealer called "The Grim Reaper"; which would constantly attempt to kill my mother. During this long period of my adolescent years, with her diagnoses, my Narcissistic father became even more frustrated and angry. His belt buckle was his tool to instill fear and authority.

My mom was admitted into several hospitals over a dozen times from 1995 to 1999. She even managed to overdose once and stop her heart by swallowing all her medications one day; luckily, it didn't kill her. Throughout these years, my mother went from doctor to doctor, desperately seeking an answer or solution. With the polarized views of many professionals, she was given a carousel of medications. She also participated in two of the most widely employed techniques in treating trauma: exposure therapy and cognitive behavioral therapy. Neither of these therapies worked. As a last-ditch effort, she was given shock treatment which had no positive results and only made her worse.

I was in a whirlwind of trauma and abuse. By the age of 16, I had developed a full-blown addiction to cocaine and had been raped four times. Two of these rapes were unrelated to Bob's abuse and degradation.

That same year I witnessed my best friend overdose and die in front of me. I had had enough. Eventually, I had an opportune moment and managed to get away from Bob completely. I ran away and never looked back.

From the age of 14 to 19 I attempted suicide approximately 18 times. When I turned 16, I recklessly ran away from everything, including school, people, and my volatile home.

Disengaged with life, I immersed myself in work and suppressed all the hurt and pain caused by so many people I trusted and loved.

I found myself leaving one bad relationship and diving into the next. I was so broken by the age of 19 that suicide always seemed to be the only option. I was incredibly tired mentally and emotionally. Eventually, it became physical. I was constantly ill, sore, sick, and panicked that I was dying of some "mystery illness". I lost count of how many emergency room visits I made when my chest would "bang" so hard I thought I was having a heart attack or worse- going to die.

There was just darkness with no light in sight. The tipping point arrived when I reached my twenties and I was tired of being tired. I was extremely angry, but it fueled something in me that was much bigger than myself. I started to accept my mother's illness and the dysfunction of my family. Next, I started to focus on my own path and goals.

At the age of 22, I met the father of my three children and thought I had finally found my movie-made love story. It was an amazing whirlwind of adoration, affection, and love. This would be what most refer to as the love bombing stage. He was charming, charismatic, funny and unlike anyone I had ever met. I was hooked!

His motivation to carrying on this love affair only lasted a couple months and ended after I became pregnant with our son in 2003. Life thereafter was hell; I was caged in a nightmare for eleven years with a narcissistic man. My reality had been distorted by gas-lighting, minimizing, manipulation and constant invalidation. Once again, I was trauma bonded. I felt chained to this man who was so emotionally, verbally, and mentally abusive that I knew I would die if I couldn't manage a way out.

My self-esteem was shattered yet my shame was sky high. I would look at the person in front of me in the mirror and only see a vague resemblance of who I once was. My life seemed so fractured. I was not allowed to work and financially held hostage. I could not dress up or even go to the store for more than fifteen minutes without being questioned. I eventually had a stroke after my daughter's birth in 2004 because the stress of it all was too much to take.

My breakthrough moment arrived on a morning in 2013, three years after the birth of our third child. I stood on the bottom floor of our home ready to hang myself off our back porch as my children played upstairs. I felt guilty for not raising them in a happy home and absolutely ashamed for not sticking up for myself. All I had known my entire life was dysfunction, yet I found myself raising my children in the same destructive environment surrounded by chaos.

I felt such shame for failing as a mother. I was convinced that I had nothing of value to bring to my children's lives. I honestly felt like they would be better off without me.

As I made a bee line for the porch to end everything, I suddenly felt the energy in the room shift drastically. The magnitude of what I was about to do hit me like a ton of bricks. Here I was feeling guilty about my failings as a mother, but I was going to leave my children to be raised by their father- my abuser?

In that moment, something inside of me, something bigger than me, louder than my need to hang myself screamed out. This was a *defining moment* for me.

I was temporarily removed from my anguish and instantly viewed my situation from an objective standpoint. I was baffled at how I had given another person such power over me...*to the point where I would leave my children without a mother?*

I broke down in tears of gratitude humbled that I was able to see exactly what I was about to do before it was too late. Then something inside of me rose up! Never again would I let myself be abused and mistreated. I would give my children a great life! I felt emboldened and powerful. "You've got this," I thought to myself. So, I waited till he left for work one morning, packed only our clothes and drove away with our children—not once looking back. As a co-parent, I did not alienate him from our children but, on that day, I broke free from his abuse.

I believe that rediscovering that you are more than your trauma and abuse is key to breaking free. This realization comes from this little light deep inside us; we all have it but, too often, it's smothered by darkness. Finding this light happens when you decide on one thing- to bet on yourself. This is called resilience. It's that lovely feature of our character that allows you to bend but not completely break; much like a tree does in the vortex of a storm. This decision forever changed my life and it's barely recognizable today.

During 2014 and 2015, I embarked on a path of healing, self-discovery, and self-love. I studied various techniques on how to work through and heal from traumatic experiences. I learned that traumatic events invade our subconscious thoughts which send us into constant fight or flight mode, therefore for years I was constantly walking into emergency rooms convinced I was dying.

My road to healing started with me connecting my mind and body as one. A wise lady named Ann Weiser wrote a book called "Focusing" which initiated my connection of the two. I applied a technique that assists your autonomic nervous system to return to a regulated state. I also practiced EFT, emotional freedom techniques, such as "tapping" which helped me focus on the "now" and to be fully present in moments of stress and anxiety.

A book written by Dr. Bessel Van Der Kolk, titled "The Body Keeps Score" was recommended by my G.P. This later became the way in which I realized that my body and mind are connected and, in order to achieve full balance, both must be aligned. I chose to use "rolfing" which is a form of massage, often noted as similar to deep tissue massage where negative energy that is blocked in your body is released. I'm convinced trauma lives in the psoas muscle and needs to be moved, so my focus went there. It's been seven years of self-discovery and self-love, re-parenting myself and tons of journaling, I now am blessed enough to help others along their own journey.

Transformation Tip

I hope that my story can inspire you to bet on yourself. As a daughter of deep darkness, if I could offer advice to anyone on this journey, it is to always remember that whatever you give meaning to in life, will be followed by an emotion and those emotions will dictate your quality of life. You are not broken; you are not your trauma. I chose to be happy; I chose to live the quality of life that I deserve. I hope my story inspires you to do the same.

As an Empath, I now coach fellow Empaths, Lightworkers and HSP's into honing into their gifts so they can find their purpose. I am also blessed enough to work with survivors of narcissistic abuse and aid them in reclaiming their life. Only now have I realized that my pain was truly my purpose and has led me into a life of fulfillment and gratitude beyond measure.

Tara Murney *is a Canadian Mother of three, partner to her best friend, stepmother, and a survivor of abuse. Blessed as an Empath, she found her gift and now wants to share it with the world by encouraging people so they can find their way beyond the black shoreline and into a life that is barely recognizable. To contact Tara, go to www.theempathwithin.com or email her at info@theempathwithin.com*

Courage to Grow
By Shiran Cohen

I was born in Israel and have lived most of my life here. I'm aware that people have varied opinions of my country, but I am not here to talk about politics: I am here to share my *Defining Moment* with you

As a child, I was exposed to many traumatic events such as war and terror. I felt hated and that people wanted to hurt me. In 1994, my 17-year-old cousin, Maya Elharar, was killed in a terrorist attack. In 2002, my 26-year-old cousin, Mor Yehuda Elraz, was killed in a collision with a terrorist. As death draws near you, nothing prepares you for or gives you an answer to the question that has plagued many (including me) for years...

Why, just because you are born in a certain place, are you hated and rejected?

Nothing is more heart-wrenching than watching parents try to live on after burying their beloved child and knowing there is nothing to help them with their pain. I had become accustomed to living a life that was shaped by violence and war. After all, I live in Israel: a country where both men and women are drafted into the military at the age of 18. Women serve two years and men serve three years of compulsory and mandatory service.

I would not exchange my time of service for anything in the world. I learned so much including self-defense, first aid, body language, awareness, and so much more.

However, pain was a part of my life. As a young adult, I had already experienced abuse and violence. I knew what it meant to feel horrible pain and have no one seem to understand. No one sees, and life goes on, so you pretend everything is good, and you prove yourself as a successful person in the eyes of society.

Despite these inner struggles, I appeared to have a storybook life. I worked for an Israeli airline company in the field of defense security and passenger safety; an "important job" that afforded me a coveted lifestyle of travel, leisure, comfort, and prestige. Flights, luxury hotels, traveling the world and getting to know new cultures were part of my daily routine.

Sometimes they would send us for a few days, weeks or even months; getting on a flight to another country was simply the way to get to work. But I loved it! I was addicted to it. Once something you do fulfills at least 3 of the 6 human needs, you become addicted to it.

According to life coach Tony Robbins, all humans have six human needs. He specifies that those 6 human needs are as follows:

1.) **Certainty**- knowing that we can avoid pain and gain pleasure
2.) **Uncertainty/Variety**- the need for the unknown, change, new stimuli
3.) **Significance**- a sense of uniqueness and importance
4.) **Connection/Love**- a strong sense of closeness or union with someone or something
5.) **Growth** - expanding capacity, ability or understanding

6.) **Contribution** - a sense of service and focus on helping, giving to, and supporting others

www.tonyrobbins.com/mind-meaning/do-you-need-to-feel-significant/

My job gave me everything I needed and fulfilled all six of the preceding needs.

In March of 2013, tragedy struck, and I was injured in a car accident. The other driver ran a red light and hit me head-on. In addition to working, I was a student studying architecture and interior design. When the accident occurred, I had just left school and was on my way home to pack my suitcase for a scheduled flight to London that evening. Instead of boarding a plane, I wound up in the hospital with broken bones.

After the fractures healed, I was still in an enormous amount of pain and was diagnosed with both PTSD (post-traumatic stress disorder) and CRPS (complex regional pain syndrome). Due to CRPS, I still always feel pain in my right hand. The impact of the mental and physical pain I experienced completely sabotaged the life path that I had envisioned for myself.

When the accident occurred, I was unable to work and lost my lifeline to fulfilling all 6 of those needs. At first, I went on a lengthy, nonpaid sick leave. Eventually, I went back to work, but the pain was too great. The accident created a circumstance in my life that I didn't know how to deal with. I felt like I was hanging by my fingertips before falling into a deep hole.

To make matters worse, a month before the accident, I had purchased my first house which was undergoing renovation. The renovation was quoted at $28,000 and quickly turned into two renovations totaling $170,000! As the renovation progressed, we found more problems that required the investment of more money and time to fix. I was drowning in debt. In fact, *all* the residual effects of the accident were swallowing me alive.

The accident affected me in the following areas:

- **Finances**: After the accident, I was buried in an enormous amount of debt. I incurred huge expenses on doctors, medical, pain clinics, physical therapy, medication, psychological therapy etc. I had spent over six figures trying to find a solution to my physical and mental pain and was still suffering!

- **Health**: In addition to PTSD and CRPS, I suffered from frequent headaches, damage to my occipital nerve, pain in my neck and back, sleep deprivation, weight gain, anxiety, high blood pressure and a weakened immune system. I felt frustrated, angry, worthless and incapable because I had lost control and lost myself. Waking up in the morning was the saddest moment of my day because it meant another day of excruciating pain with the knowledge that tomorrow wouldn't be any different.

- **Relationships**: I began pushing away anyone who tried to get close to me because I was so ashamed of what I had become. I allowed everyone to think I was okay, but I was angry and irritable often.

My pain cost me that much! And I lived six years of my life in this state of suffering.

Eventually, I realized that my hopelessness was fueling this cycle of defeat. I began to realize that I had to take ownership of my life before I could change it.

Accepting this inevitable truth was a *defining moment* for me because it was like someone placed the keys to unlock my full potential in my hand. It was only after I accepted my circumstances as my own, instead of fighting them, that I felt authorized to change them.

I had to believe that I would see better days before I could manifest them in my life. I choose to believe and took the steps necessary to gain the tools to make a change. I began an extensive process of self-assessment and personal development. I sought to understand and learn as much as I could.

I began to read, study, listen to podcasts and attend masterminds in pursuit of knowledge.

The cliché that knowledge is power still rings true. Knowledge is power and I set out on a quest to acquire the tools needed to radically change my life. As I learned different strategies for success in the areas of finances, emotional health, physical health and relationships, I began to apply them to my own life. I stuck with the processes that worked for me and modified or abandoned the ones that didn't. I began creating my own habits and rituals.

Today, I am happy and thriving! My life has completely transformed since my defining moment in the following areas:

- **Finances**: I graduated school, found an amazing new job and increased my knowledge about money (and applied it). I started a business and created multiple streams of income.

- **Health**: I changed my nutrition and gradually began to exercise. I maintained these rituals as a lifestyle and lost 44 pounds in just eight short months! My blood pressure stabilized and the pain and frequency of my headaches, neckaches and backaches decreased significantly. Under medical supervision, I was able to go from taking eight pain pills per day to not taking any. My immune system improved, and I no longer got sick every two weeks. Since I changed my diet and added exercise to my weekly routine, my body is so much healthier! I still suffer from CRPS, but the pain level is now only at a three while previously it was at a seven.

- **Mentally**: I got to know myself. Meditating every day improved my body and mind. It caused me to become more aware of my feelings and emotions. Mindset taught me to overcome fears and past events. I was able to create goals and manage my thoughts. I'm more energetic, happy, worthy, and capable. For the first time in my life, I love the life I'm living and who I have become.

- **Relationships**: I allow people to get to know the authentic "me". Once they do, I no longer doubt their love or think, "Well, you only love what you see; believe me, you wouldn't stay around if you knew everything." Today, I love myself and others. I can also confidently say that people love me in return. My heart has grown 100 times and it's the best feeling in the world!

I am calm, attentive, understanding, patient, and have learned about human behavior more than I knew before.

Transformation Tip

The following is my advice to anyone who feels like they are "stuck" in a cycle of defeat and living a life that they desperately want to change:

1. Understand what you want and need then learn to change your habits and actions to achieve it.
2. Manage your fears and feelings to overcome the past.
3. Invest in yourself! Learn personal growth and mindset and look for the knowledge that will give you the success you want.
4. Nutrition and Exercise. You only have one body; take care of it!
5. Seek advice only from those who have achieved what you want.

Shiran *served two years in the Israeli military and 10+ years of defense work preventing terrorism in aviation worldwide, where she received a Certificate of Excellence in the role.*

Shiran has visited many countries and has vigorously studied human behavior, body language, self-defense and many other tools. Shiran coaches people all over the world on Non-Verbal skills and techniques to help businesses & entrepreneurs develop their body language skills so they can have a SMART ADVANTAGE communicating the right marketing message, brilliantly negotiate in sales, and become effective in their business.

She is also a #1 international bestselling author of the book Become Brilliant: Roadmap From Fear to Courage. She currently helps entrepreneurs develop their body language skills so they can have a smart advantage communicating the right marketing message, brilliantly negotiate in sales, and become effective in their business.

Shiran is also a trainer for Tony Robbins and Dean Graziosi on their KBB (Knowledge Broker Blueprint) workshops.

If you desire to transform your life and would like to learn more about her book or program, email Shiran at Shiran.public@gmail.com

Join her free Facebook group:

SMART ADVANTAGE Entrepreneurs Body Language-Marketing & Negotiation Skills

When the Only Way Out is Through...

By Karen Loenser

My grandmother was a wise woman who lived a lot of life and was always armed with a reassuring phrase that could soothe almost any fear or challenge. When things got particularly tough, she'd call on her favorite piece of advice and say, "Well dear, sometimes, the only way out is through." Back then, it struck me a trite, old school phrase, but as I look back now on our family's story of survival, I know for sure that "the through" can be both a challenge and reward. The "through" can change your life forever.

The automatic doors of the hospital sprang open like a mechanical hand snatching us from the serene normalcy of our everyday lives into the vast, controlled chaos of the ER. It was mid-January, and we arrived on a grey, somber morning. Inside those doors, there was no turning back. It was the start of our journey "through."

We pulled off our jackets and grabbed the last remaining chairs in the waiting room. My husband, Ralph, approached the admissions desk. When the receptionist asked if we had been there before, Ralph nodded; our 8-

month-old son Graham's information had already become a fixture in their database.

I had given birth in this hospital. Nearing the age of forty, I was one of those "older pregnant moms," requiring extra OB visits and fussy monitoring of vitals. Spotting in my early pregnancy, required a 2-week break from my hectic pace at work. But things quickly normalized, and I was in good standing for my "so-called age."

Near my due date, I experienced a sudden surge of dizziness. I sat to catch my breath and dialed my husband, "I think you should get checked," he said firmly, but not overly alarmed.

At the OB's office, the nurse explained that my blood pressure had spiked. "Time to admit you," she said. I was sent home to pack and ordered to arrive early the next morning to the hospital.

At 7:06 pm on March 23, 2001, my beautiful boy was placed on my belly. Ralph beamed with pride as he cut the umbilical cord. With joyful relief, we swaddled his healthy, hearty, little body and gave thanks. I watched Ralph follow the nurse down the hallway to give him his first bath, as the doctor finished up on me.

And that's when things went horribly wrong...

"We need you to come back Karen...squeeze my hand if you can hear me." Somewhere far away, I heard Ralph whispering in my ear; trying to wake me.

I was so tired. My body felt too heavy to move but his urgency pulled me out of my grogginess. When I opened my eyes, I saw my tearful husband standing over me. When I tried to speak, my voice caught in my throat...

"You're on a breathing tube honey...try not to talk."

I was confused...what was I doing there? My last memory was giving birth to my son. The joy of seeing his beautiful face...

Oh my God...I panicked, where is my baby???

As if reading my mind, Ralph said, "The baby is fine honey. He's with your Mom downstairs. You're in the ICU. You've been here for days-you gave us all quite a scare."

After delivery I had hemorrhaged and ended up with emergency surgery and a series of blood transfusions that saved my life. For days afterwards, I was in an induced coma, saved I am certain by the deep love of my husband and family, as well as a steady stream of Reiki healers, arranged by my vigilant Mother, who worked on me while I slept.

Days later, we went home, and things slowly returned to normal. We named our son "Graham". Graham was an amazing soul that quickly grew into a precocious ball of smiles. Healthy, happy, thriving...

Until he wasn't.

In early November, our babysitter Dora, called me at work. "Miss Karen, little Grahamie has been throwing up again. I think he should get looked at by the doctor." We had been alternating from breast milk to formula and a newer regime of food, which seemed to have triggered a series of stomach issues.

I knew it couldn't be a virus since Dora hadn't taken him out of the house in weeks. We had just gotten through the madness of 9/11 and, living outside of Manhattan in a New Jersey suburb, we wanted him to stay close to home.

The Pediatrician affirmed that his new diet was the culprit. He suggested some alternatives but, three weeks later, I was back with similar issues only Graham had a fever this time. The doctor didn't seem alarmed and instructed me to come back if things worsened. In my mind, I heard the siren of a mother's instinct begin to bellow a loud cry of warning. But for what?

I didn't know.

Graham continued to yoyo between seemingly normal health and bouts of vomiting. In early January, I'd planned a surprise 40th birthday party for

Ralph and my Mom came to help. She hadn't seen Graham in a few weeks and pulled me aside to say, "Karen, you have to get him to another doctor. When did he get that bump on his head?"

What bump? Suddenly, I saw the small lump on his forehead and was terrified. We trusted Dora implicitly, and knew she would have told us if he had fallen. We immediately took Graham to the ER.

As we waited, Grahams fever climbed. He was listless and dehydrated. During Graham's examination, the doctor noticed his rigid belly and stated that the bump on his head could be symptomatic of a few causes, including a brain tumor. He ordered a spinal tap and Cat Scan. We waited in agony for the results.

A nurse who helped deliver Graham walked by as we waited. Ralph recognized her and remembered the kindness she had shown him as he waited in the ICU. "I can't believe, after all of that drama, you are back here again," she said. "I know the angels must be looking out for you though. You are a strong family."

As if on cue, hours later, our family's strength would be tested. The results indicated that our son had stage four neuroblastoma; a one in a million cancer, that primarily affects young children. Graham had a tumor about the size of a lemon in his adrenal gland. The cancer had spread to his bones, including his skull, thus causing the bump on his head. He needed immediate surgery to remove the tumor, another to implant a portacath, followed by rounds of chemotherapy. We were told to go to Tomorrows Children Cancer Treatment Center at Hackensack Medical Hospital to meet with a team of pediatric oncologists immediately.

What followed was arguably my lowest point as a mother.

I had always feared cancer. I feared it when my young aunt lost her life to lung cancer, when my mother-in-law and sister-in-law battled breast cancer and when my husband spoke of his father's death from cancer which occurred when he was a toddler.

No dear God in heaven, my infant son has cancer? You can't ask that of me.

That is THE THING, I cannot do.

And yet, there it was.

As the doctor provided his diagnosis, I held Graham's limp, sleeping body in my arms and went inwardly numb. I felt my heart physically stop. I felt the fear sear like lightning bolts through my veins. Like that moment in the ICU, my voice was caught in my throat. An inward scream of "NOOOO!!! I can't do this!" slashed through my heart. I placed Graham in his father's arms and said, "My son is going to die," and ran out of the room.

My mother followed me down the hall. "Karen, this is an unbelievable situation. We're all scared but Graham needs you and I know you can do this. You can."

Behind her, was my ever-strong, courageous husband. Who held our son and said, "Karen, we are going to get through this. We will do this together. He is going to be fine."

I looked at my little boy who still managed to smile through his pain and sickness then stretched his little arms back to me for a hug of reassurance. "Okay," I said, "Let's do this."

The following weeks of treatment were a blur. Of cradling his weak head while nurses ran an IV from his skull because he was so dehydrated that they couldn't find a vein. Of placing his tiny body on the operating table and leaving him in the hands of masked strangers. Of sleeping upright night after night. Of waiting for news on how each round of chemo was impacting the prognosis of our precious little boy.

Numerous moments tested our faith in the months that followed. White cell counts that were too low or too high. Fevers that spiked in the middle of the night requiring late night ambulance rides to the ER. But we also proved that the ICU nurse was indeed right about our family. We were a strong unit. We became good at keeping charts, and check-in lists, and action plans. Of being the watchdog and protector of anything and anyone that touched our child. We questioned the so-called medical authorities and double checked every prescription script and diagnosis. We lived in the moment. We prayed all the time. We slept in increments. But we never spoke of the possibility of Graham dying ever again.

And that was how we took our power back. This shift in perspective was a *defining moment* for us because it gave us the inner strength that we needed to be strong for our son.

What we learned has never left us. We learned to trust in things seen and unseen. We opened to alternative medicines like Reike and Gin Shin, and holistic modalities to enhance Graham's recovery outside of conventional medicine. We learned about energy healing, and positive thinking. We looked for angels everywhere. We visualized and affirmed that Graham was well. We opened our hearts and minds to the kindness of strangers. We learned to live in the moment; truly the toughest lesson for two madly controlling corporate parents, who wanted to use our management skills to create the project plan around our child's recovery. Graham reminded us to play. We savored every moment. Our family unit reigned. We were a force of love to be reckoned with.

I received a card during Graham's illness that had a quote from The Course in Miracles that said, "A miracle is a shift in perception from fear to love." Inside the card, was another quote that said, "If you knew who walked beside you at all times, you would never experience fear or doubt ever again."

I re-read those words often. They came true for us.

Graham recently graduated from high school. He doesn't remember a lot about those trips to the hospital, but we share the stories and the photos with him every year on his cancer-free birthday which ironically happens every September 11th. He will always be, a living, breathing miracle.

Today, we live on the other side of the dark tunnel and share our story with other parents who have and are still facing their fears with all the courage they can muster. We tell them to hold on tight and keep their eyes on the light. We tell them that it is love that will get them "through."

Transformation Tip

The diagnosis is not your prognosis. The diagnosis may define the disease, but the prognosis is only a forecast of outcome- it is NOT fact or fate.

Your biggest life challenge, your most incomprehensible fear, can be the very thing that shows you your purpose – what you have come into this world to do. When you are most afraid, close your eyes and focus only on love...let it fill you and surround you. There you will find the heart of your soul, your endless resource of power and strength.

You are braver and more powerful than you know, and when you get through this (and you will), you will find the life map of your soul.

Karen Loenser *is an award-winning TV producer, digital strategist, podcast host, writer, intuitive and workshop developer, who is obsessed with finding new mediums to create and share stories to uplift our souls. In addition to this book, Karen is also releasing her new book "LifeMapping: Decoding the Blueprint of Your Soul," through Defining Moments Press. For more info, please email karen_loenser@discovery.com*

Making Health and Happiness a #1 Priority
By Keri Faith Knudtson

There I was basking in the pillow of comfort on my full-sized mattress that engulfed me in a sea of discomfort.

I sat there tucked into a ball. The box of Kleenex next to me on the dresser and more than half of its used contents spread over the bedspread. It was 1:00pm. I knew at some point I would have to get out of bed and take a shower, but my body was melted into the mattress and overwhelmed by the warmth of my sheets.

My internal pain and sadness were comforted by knowing that I had nothing to do that day. Idleness had become a way of life for me. That's because I knew that my mood wasn't going to flip anytime soon. This had been going on for months, ever since the days shortened and the nights grew longer while the temperatures dropped outside. I was going to get zero accomplished today.

It was cold and cloudy outside, the sun barely shining brought more sorrow and tears to my face. I thought to myself, "If only the sun was out, I would feel so much better." My stomach growled since I hadn't eaten since the previous day's dinner. My lack of desire and drive to wake and transition into alertness was stronger than my will to drag myself out of bed and eat.

Depression is dark and ominous. It is an ever-present pain that feels unending. It creates waves and swells of negativity in one's thoughts, feelings, and emotions. It transforms an ordinary life into an extraordinarily debilitating one of suffering and sacrificed time, health, and happiness. It replaces all that is good with loss, sickness, and misery. Too many great souls have been lost to depression. Yet, as twisted as it sounds, it was my comfort zone. The comfort of my home, bed, and emotional distress came with the cycles of the seasons.

Every October, once the sun began to sink lower towards the horizon, I was overcome with tears, pain, lack of motivation, internal negative self-talk, and a sense of overall failure and misery. It was like clockwork- just like a menstrual cycle. I did not have to look at the calendar to know that the season of depression was upon me with the heaviness of thoughts and emotions that drowned me.

Seasonal depression came over me like a blanket engulfing my heart. My once happy and energized self from June and July was shipped away to sea and the tears of desperation, isolation, loneliness, darkness, and lack of interest in the world flooded every cell in my body.

How does this happen? Why do I feel this way every year? What will I have to do to survive the next long six months that will drag on until the rebirth of spring blooms?

In one way or another, each person on earth will experience pain, negativity, or a few days, weeks, or months associated with depression. Whether or not a person should seek professional help is largely determined by the length of time and intensity of the negative feelings they are experiencing.

In my case, my upbringing was filled with pain, suffering, and disengagement from society because of my lack of clarity around the sadness within me. I didn't identify the depression and was not focused on the goodness that was buried inside that nobody witnessed around me. I had severe and debilitating anxiety about leaving my home, going to school, socializing with friends and even family. I felt different and never really fit in any box or circle. I loved to be alone, and still do, yet was not sure why or what caused me to be so disengaged in life.

As I grew into adolescence, my coping mechanisms transformed to using alcohol and drugs to escape the painful reality I experienced daily. The reality was all self-induced but the more I learned about past generations, I heard more and more talk of illnesses that ran deep in my blood.

First with my paternal grandfather who was a genius in his own right. He attended Georgia Tech until the Great Depression hit and migrated west to Los Angeles, California. While in Los Angeles, he became a thriving Engineer and went on to create and patent the adjustable stop countersink filing his patent on July 14, 1941. Unfortunately, he later experienced and suffered from schizophrenia. He withdrew from being a successful contributor to society because of societal norms and the misconception of how to deal with mental health. In and out of electronic shock therapies, he was a product of the stigma associated with such disease.

I still hear references about his life and the way he chose to live the latter 40 years of it as having an 'unhealthy mind'. I question if he was truly "unhealthy" or if he was a brilliant soul dissociated with some of its greatest strengths despite having failures and setbacks. Was it his belief or the world's belief in what a healthy, successful, and thriving male in the 1960s was supposed to portray? Maybe it was not anything more than a soul so large and grand that did not fit into a typical box or circle. Now from being on the other side of depression, and transforming my own "unhealthy mind," I see the disconnect from the past that is sometimes misunderstood in the present.

I have seen it and still do with my own eyes, the mistreatment of those with mental health struggles. I was determined throughout my 20s that I was not going to be subject to mistreatment by society, so I was quiet and removed. I stayed silent. The silence was feeding the darkness. Yet, my self-portrayal in the external world did not match that of my internal struggles.

I became a really good actress putting on a show of being happy and content because the world doesn't like to see or hear about pain. Learning to smile was the only thing that made me a 'normal functioning' contributor in society. Although the silence continued, because depression was portrayed by society as something which needed to be hidden from the world.

When I was away at college out of state from my California home at the University of Colorado in Boulder, I was subject to an abundance of freedom to mask my pain and escape from the past. Yet, I was escaping farther and farther from reality while making my own reality. My own reality was filled with destructive behaviors, unhealthy relationships, negative self-talk, and other daily habits that did not help a college student to thrive, let alone a depressed one.

The second semester arrived during my second year of college. While taking a course called Meditation, I was introduced to a psychotherapist who guided us as a guest speaker. This was a significant moment for me as I connected with her on a psyche level and knew she was the answer to my cry for help.

It was February and just a few months prior I had proclaimed to my parents that I was suffering from depression and was told to, "Snap out of it." I was determined to not settle for this answer because I knew a life-long battle for happiness was not something I was going to magically fix, but a life-long journey was going to begin. At this moment, I began to not just settle but strive for constant and never-ending improvement. Once something is declared to the universe, the universe responds with a message or moment to learn from. What this therapist introduced to me during the meditation course was the answer I was looking for.

I immediately looked her up after that guided meditation and scheduled a session with her which led to another guided mediation with lots of questioning, answering, and tears shed. She explained things to me, about me, that I never quite understood but made perfect sense. She guided me to answers, to the reasons WHY, and to continued growth and healing. That summer I took meditation workshops, continued therapy, and the summer sun and energy nullified that once hopeless existence I felt just six months prior. I have forgotten her name, but I will always remember the message she delivered.

That year was 1997 and I was not just introduced to meditation, but to traditional Western psychiatry. Consequently, I was prescribed my first anti-depressant because this seemed to be the solution to every problem in the modern western 20th Century world, and still is a default treatment frequently used today to soothe depression.

The medication provided minimal change although the side effects provided measurable pitfalls. I didn't like taking them but was told it was going to help so I did. I placed my belief in the doctor treating me and the modern practices but resonated more heavily in the ancient rituals of spirituality and mediation from my therapist. Then, something miraculous happened in summertime; I reached a peaceful and content state.

October came quickly falling down and the once motivated individual I began to love was packed away for the winter. The medication was now necessary (according to the professionals) as the answer to my darkness. And, for the next ten years, I lived by a prescription list that was an entire page long; a list that perfectly outlined the array of medications that were to heal my wounded mind, body and soul. I didn't deviate from following my check list of required medications until a sunny, bright day in October just a few months after my blissful summer wedding.

On this particular day, I sat in the bathroom with a pregnancy test in hand and two bright pink strips glaring at me with a piercing message of change on the horizon: I was pregnant.

While most women would be ecstatic and shed tears of joy, I was immediately shedding tears of sadness and disbelief. How was I going to bear a child? What was I going to do? Why is this happening to me?

I never thought I would be a mother, but most messages arrive from the universe to teach us something. I learned over the next year how to embrace change and transform into a better version of myself. I discovered how to survive free from medications, drugs, and alcohol and let go of the limiting beliefs and stories I had from the past that no longer served me.

The birth of my son was a *defining moment* for me because it changed the standard I held for my life and the self-perception of what I was capable of. As I brought him home from the hospital, I realized I could no longer just barely survive because another human was dependent on me to grow and thrive. At that exact moment, I traded the "I" in my illness for a "we" and that's when my lifelong journey to wellness began.

I had a strong new WHY to live and transform from where I was to who I always yearned to be: a healthy thriving high-achieving individual. It took a mere moment in time to shift the belief around my purpose in the world. It does not require a lifetime to cure a lifelong problem. For me, it was a split second in time where I saw the defining moment glare me in the eyes through my son's existence.

During the next ten years of my life, I repeated the same processes to achieve my dreams and goals. Each time I wanted something new, to reach a new level of success and accomplishment, I applied the same methods and frameworks. After one of my biggest accomplishments in 2018, graduating college with a Bachelor of Arts in Psychology, I knew a "lifelong" journey to wellness wasn't necessary, but the frameworks, strategies, structure, and key attributes that had produced positive results were. They are built on a system and standards in one's mindset, conscious and subconscious programming.

I realized if I don't guide others on the fast track, I'd be doing the world a disservice and letting my full potential go to waste. Now I dedicate my days to serving others in personal development thought mindset coaching, keynote speaking, online Masterminds, and providing guidance through Masterminds and the Keri Faith on Purpose Podcast.

Had I not found my way to wellness through the defining moment of creating my "WHY", I would not have the opportunity to guide others to live a happier and healthier life. It takes a simple shift to make a transformation long lasting and sustainable.

Transformation Tip

If you feel like your life's circumstances are making you depressed, feel hopeless or helpless, here is a good way to change your perspective quickly. With practice, it will become a healthy habit that can provide you with hope, optimism, and a desired result that energizes you to move forward instead of staying stuck where you are. I refer to M.I.N.D. set as **M**anaging **I**nternal **N**egative **D**ialogue and the process to manage it is termed the A, B, C's of Positive Mindset.

Here are the 7-steps to creating positive change for long-lasting sustained health and happiness:

- A=Adversity (Current negative circumstance, feelings, or emotions)
- B=Belief (What is your current thought about the adversity?)
- C=Circumstance (Or Result/Outcome)
- If you are not happy with your current circumstance or result or outcome, move onward.

- **D**=Disassociate or Disengage (You are not your feelings, emotions, results, or outcomes because they are always changing and evolving. Place it in a box and look from the outside in).
- **E**=Evaluate (Look at the 'B' = Belief in the box)
- **F**=Frame (Look at the belief from multiple perspectives. Reframe it. Ask other people's opinions of the situation if you need help doing so from a neutral viewpoint.)
- **G**=Gratitude (Reframe the belief with gratitude. Focus on what you do have versus what you do not have. Make gratitude a habit and the 'Circumstances' are most likely to change when your default 'Belief' changes and is replaced with being thankful and grateful.

My depression was a gift, and it was the pain that is now my purpose to help others.

Keri Faith Knudtson *is an Author, Speaker, Podcast Host, and Coach supporting the harmony between mind, body, and soul's purpose aligning it with one's personal and professional life. Author of Pillars to Positivity, Podcast host of Keri Faith on Purpose and Keynote Speaker specializing in mindset, personal and self-development, while incorporating spiritual wisdom for long term sustained health, happiness, and well-being. She connects, creates, and transforms lives from the inside out. Join the FREE Facebook group* https://www.facebook.com/groups/positivemindsetmasters, *follow her on Instagram* https://instagram.com/kerifaithonpurpose *or email* kerifaithonpurpose@gmail.com

2

Ultimate Survival

It is Easy for Me to Take the Next Step

By Heidi Nye

Throughout my life, I've had challenges. Type 1 insulin-dependent diabetes since age 13 and all the medical adventures that that entails. Coronary disease since 2000. A few heart attacks, but, because my responses are a bit dulled and chest pain or pressure is ever-present, I just continued. I worked an entire day, not knowing I was in dire straits because it was just a bit more chest pain than usual.

In 2008, my kidneys failed. I went on dialysis which I did in my bedroom instead of a clinic, because I wanted to be responsible for my own care. This was 10 hours a day (at minimum) and up to 14 hours per day, hooked up to a machine.

A tube surgically inserted into the peritoneum, the sack that holds the organs. Eighteen inches of the tube protruded from my tummy. I connected the end of the tube to the dialysis machine. That tubing, plus an insulin pump and a continuous blood sugar monitor, was a lot of gear to hide under my clothes!

I was so weak that I could barely cross a room some days. I continued to teach journalism at Cal State, Long Beach, until the end of the semester because I had contracted to do so. I then went on disability retirement. For the next five and a half years, I survived on my pension of $600 a month—meager because I retired early—plus Social Security disability of $1,000. $1,600 a month is a real challenge in Southern California. When I was able, I wrote articles for magazines and edited dissertations to make ends meet.

You aren't automatically placed on the transplant wait list once your kidneys fail. First, I had to be permitted on the list. A group of doctors from my health care plan, doctors I never saw or talked with, nixed my application. When people say there are no such things as death panels, they obviously haven't had their kidneys fail.

I immediately asked my nephrologist, "What's my next step?" He said I could talk with a transplant surgeon at UCLA.

For that appointment, I dressed in a gray wool suit and brought along my published books and articles. Perhaps 60 people were in the waiting room, all with their significant others. I was the only patient flying solo. But unlike them, I dressed as if for a job interview and projected strength. I pinched my cheeks to bring color to my face and to look as healthy as possible. I wanted to present as a person deserving to live. I was there to make a pitch for my life.

The surgeon, however, turned me down because of my co-morbidities. That is, the other things that could put me six feet under.

Without skipping a beat, I asked to talk with the head of the department. The surgeon was shocked by my assertiveness but went to get him. The head surgeon and I had a lovely chat, some of it in German. I looked at him straight on and said, "I KNOW I will do well with a transplant. Give me a chance."

But first I had to get my heart in shape. That meant triple bypass surgery and months of rehabilitation.

I had the surgery and asked friends to help me once I got home. No one showed up to cook a meal, mop my floors, or do the laundry. Most people didn't even respond to my email or just replied with something like "Chin up!" or "I'm not very good at housework." My son helped when he could, but he was working two jobs: one with a commute to LA.

Though my friends' lack of response saddened me, in time I forgave them, knowing that most people are deathly afraid of death, and, since I was on the precipice of death, they wished to avoid me.

Plus, people always come to me for help. If I was impaired, then they feared they were even more vulnerable.

I had to remember that I am very fortunate that I have faced death so many times, and most people have not had a single brush with it.

I did the laundry myself, carrying a few items to the wash machine at a time until I had a full load, resting in between. I mopped the floor by pushing around a wet rag with my foot.

I ignored doctors' orders to refrain from driving for six weeks following triple bypass. I was back behind the wheel in less than ten days.

As someone with a degree in philosophy and as a former journalist, I want the truth. Here are the facts:

Maybe 10% of all dialysis patients make the transplant wait list. Of those, 50% die within five years on dialysis, and half the rest are taken off the list because their health deteriorates to a point at which they couldn't survive surgery. Of the remaining 2.5%, the wait time was ten years in LA for a deceased donor.

I embraced those facts and looked at the very real possibility of never getting off dialysis and dying in the next few years. That acceptance was liberating. A *defining moment* for me really. After releasing all negative thinking, I was able to concentrate my energy fully on taking the steps to attain a transplant and prevent my death.

While on dialysis, I was in the emergency room a dozen times and hospitalized a few more, and had multi-directional vertigo, anemia, water retention, an infection in the tubing, triple bypass surgery, and a heart attack. I broke my femur twice while being filmed in New York City for an HBO special on the shortage of kidney donors.

While filming, I fell from a standing position. A healthy person would have simply gotten back up and brushed the dirt off her skirt. But my bones were so brittle that my femur broke, then broke again in the hospital when I tripped on the cords around my bed.

Plus, I had to move my mother to California from Wisconsin, personally handling the sale of her possessions, the packing, and the search for an assisted living facility. I lived in a 400-square-foot apartment with my dog and, at that time, my son, too. There was no room for her.

She was failing big time, and my brother who lived 30 miles away in Milwaukee had disowned her years prior. She was in her early 80's and addicted to pain meds with the anxiety-ridden personality which that entails. Caring for her when I was struggling to care for myself was daunting.

The last time I saw her, she yelled and cursed at me to get away, finally voicing what I had always suspected she felt. Yet, I also wondered if she even knew who I was. That night, while hooked up to the dialysis machine, I received a call from a local hospital, saying that my mother had lost consciousness and was on life support. She had a DNR on file, but somehow the night staff hadn't read her request.

No boyfriend or husband. It's been a mystery why men aren't knocking down my door. A tall, slender blonde with blue eyes, a credit score of 821, a certified massage therapist with 20 years of professional experience, who can do dry wall and hold up her end of the conversation on any subject except sports, consumer goods, and pop culture.

In high school, I asked six boys to prom. All six gave me firm no's on the spot.

To love someone with all my heart and be loved richly and deeply in return is an experience I would welcome any time. With all this going on, it would have been wonderful to have had a partner during those years.

My existence was often mind over matter. Ascending just a few stairs I would whisper to myself, "It is easy for me to climb these steps." And when walking, "It is easy for me to take the next step."

In truth, I was struggling. But I kept climbing stairs and walking and projecting a strong image to the world.

After quite a few adventures in medicine, I received a kidney from a living donor—Brandi, a 30-year-old manager of a repo firm. I have one tough kidney.

Part of a donor chain. A man in Philadelphia walked into a clinic and said he wanted to donate to whomever was top of the list and compatible. So, he gave to a man in Thousand Oaks, his wife Brandi gave to me, my Buddhist neighbor gave to someone in North Carolina, and that person's friend or family member gave to someone in San Francisco. A total miracle of trust because, at each juncture, a donor was free to drop out.

I took myself off all pain meds the morning after surgery, started doing laps around the ward, and petitioned to be released a day earlier than any UCLA transplant patient ever had been released before.

I had some glitches in my recovery, but eventually returned to the world and founded a magazine. My first gig after disability.

I didn't start that journey with money in the bank or sales experience or a supportive spouse or anything to fall back on.

Sixty-eight presentations to make my first sale. Nine months to get above baseline. No income for nine months because I was off Social Security as soon as I was working. So, I slept in my living room on the floor and rented out my bedroom on Airbnb. It was either that or give up my apartment and live out of my car.

Staying alive still takes a lot of my time, a minimum of 15 hours a week with lab tests, doctor visits, insulin pump tech support, all kinds of hoops to jump through. I've had emergency room visits, surgeries, and hospitalizations since the transplant. My son moved to Pennsylvania over eight years ago; no boyfriend or husband yet, but my sweet, little dog Rasputin is still a good boy.

Just as when I was going through dialysis and surgeries, I am thankful for all that I have. A working kidney, a roof over my head, a good son though now at a distance, the best dog ever. A million little things too. New paint on my walls, healthy plants in my windowsill, pleasant conversations with strangers, the comfort that comes from holding a hot cup of tea in my hands and breathing in the steam.

All because I took the next step.

You can too.

Transformation Tip

When you are in a difficult situation, make peace with the worst that can happen. Otherwise, worry and fear will immobilize you at the very time when you need all your energy to work toward what you do want to occur.

Heidi Nye has worked as a writer and editor throughout her career: everything from a Los Angeles Times reporter, author of a book on traditional Chinese medicine, and West Coast correspondent for an HVAC magazine to essayist, travel writer, and award-winning poet, and many points in between. She is currently finishing up a collection of short stories and working on a novel. She is always looking for new assignments and can be reached at SurroundedByBeauty@YMail.com.

The Reality of Life With an Eating Disorder

By Devyn Faz

My life changed for the worst the summer of my sophomore year of high school. Just like all teenagers, summer vacation consisted of sleeping through to the afternoon and hanging out with friends. While most kids my age slept in because there was nothing else to do or they needed to rest and rejuvenate for the next day, I used sleep for a more destructive purpose. My shocking truth was that I used sleep as a method to take away my hunger cues when I first started skipping meals. It's ironic that sleep, something so vital to one's life, changed my life and health for the worse.

I grew up as a dancer. My mom enrolled me into my very first dance class at the age of two years young and I developed an eager passion for the sport that no one can take away. As active as I was, my food intake and calorie outtake never occurred to me. I was able to enjoy my favorite fast food restaurants without worrying about my body image because I saw myself as active.

Even the revealing dance costumes that I wore through my whole dance career never changed my eating habits. For fifteen years, I was carefree about food and eating was the highlight of my day! My school day would end at three o' clock and I was eager to devour my next meal. To be quite honest, I was never on a quest to lose weight. In fact, the journey to my weight loss was initially accidental.

My battle simply began when I was bombarded with compliments such as "Did you lose weight?" "You look good; what have you been doing?" While I never noticed my unexpected weight loss, the compliments were fuel to continuing the bad habits.

As strange as it might sound, receiving these compliments made something click in my mind...*if I'm not awake for long periods of time, I won't consume as much food.* It was twisted logic, but the showering of compliments served as incentive to continue on with this behavior. As I started to consume fewer calories, my appetite began to shrink. And since my body no longer beckoned me to eat, my motivation to eat deteriorated and I just kept dropping weight. My meals soon began to look like toddler portions, and coffee.

I began searching the internet for low calorie foods and methods of burning excessive amounts of calories at home. My body was in a deficit but, when I looked in the mirror, my body dysmorphia said to keep going. The bags under my eyes from a lack of nutrients said you can cover it with makeup. The brittleness of my nails was easily disguised with nail polish. I knew the destruction that could result from an inconsistency of eating, but I was oblivious to anything and everything except maintaining my protruding ribs and hip bones.

I would feel incredibly nauseous from not eating all day, or not eating after I regurgitated the only meal that I allowed myself to have that day. I justified this risky behavior by telling myself that it wasn't "so bad" because I was still eating *sometimes*. I kept reminding myself that the feeling would go away in college, because the lack of privacy in the dorm's communal bathroom would prevent me from throwing up my food and revealing my dark secret.

I was willing to go to great lengths so that I might achieve the grand prize of being considered "attractive" by society's rigid and unattainable standards. Only then would I consider myself valuable.

I was brainwashed, like so many people, into believing that achieving the "perfection" that I so often saw on TV would make me happy. I didn't consider that this perceived perfection is manufactured and often a result of makeup, airbrushing, crash and starvation diets, and cosmetic surgery. My life consisted of regimented rules that I had created to my own detriment to achieve this standard. Thankfully, the war within my mind and body ended sooner than expected.

I vividly remember the day my recovery journey started - Sunday, September 8th. It was the day after my seventeenth birthday. On this day, I followed my usual Sunday routine. I arrived at church at 9:00 a.m. to volunteer, followed by sitting in service at 10:00 a.m. I drove straight home as soon as service let out. Immediately when I walked into my home, there was tension. I greeted my household and went to my room to find myself drowning in my social media addiction.

Not long after, my mom came into my room and by the looks of her disappointed face, I knew something was wrong. I was bombarded by questions, and I consistently denied the disordered eating habits I was accused of. "Why did your stepfather find thrown up food in your bathtub?" And that was the sentence that changed my life for the better. I broke down in tears and revealed the battle I had been facing for over a year. Anorexia nervosa and bulimia nervosa. Through what seemed like mother/daughter telepathy, I felt my mother's heart shatter into pieces. The endless tears running down her cheek. Her first born baby was facing a deadly mental illness all while discretely hiding it so no one would know the key to my 40 pound weight loss. Most people assume that eating disorders are simply a physical illness, but they are rooted by psychological thoughts.

In shock, my mother walked out of my room to find me the help I needed. This was a *defining moment* for me and the start of my healing journey. She called my biggest support system - my aunt Janie. My aunt and I have always had a strong and unique bond largely because she stepped in to help raise me when I was very young after my parents divorced.

As a single father, my father worked tireless hours to support us. His work shift started at 6:00 a.m. so I had no one to take me to school in the mornings. My aunt took me under her wing and treated me like the daughter she never had. She got me ready each morning which was no easy task - I refused to go to school without my hair curled and my outfit styled by Justice. She transported me to and from dance, took me shopping, and took on the responsibility of caring for me to the extremity of me sitting in her master's degree class. Although the two of us had an unbreakable bond,

I still never found the courage to tell her the severe conditions I was putting my body through in order to fit in with society's stereotype of "pretty".

Eating disorders have a way of tearing at your most precious relationships because so much effort and deception goes into concealing your secret. I didn't want to worry her and, frankly, I didn't want her to intervene.

A couple of phone calls and tears later, my mom came into my room to tell me I had my first appointment with a therapist who specialized in eating disorders the following afternoon. As a competitive cheerleader and dancer, I often felt judged by the outside. I selfishly was not ready to give up the body I crafted by starving and throwing up. I was not ready to see the number on the scale increase.

I had become dependent on the triggering compliments I so often received. Comments like, "You look so good; how did you lose the weight?" When I gazed in the mirror and caught sight of my emaciated frame, I felt driven and in control. I feared gaining weight. My self-esteem was as delicate as a house of cards - one swift move and the entire structure would come tumbling down.

When the day of my first session came, I dreaded walking into the building where the session would take place. Having to go to therapy felt like the end of the world to me, yet it ended up being the best thing I could have done. In the moment of my session, I was tense and anxious. I didn't know what the future held for me.

On the outside, I was smiling because I had skipped my breakfast and lunch that morning, and I felt like I was in control of a part of my life. I neglected to see that I was one step closer to devaluing and eliminating years of my life. My eating disorder was so severe that I could fast for more than 24 hours all while having the ability to purge my food three times each day. I was vulnerable to compromised health issues such as heart failure, metabolic shut down, irreversible damage to my intestines from the abuse of laxatives, damage to my teeth and esophagus, and a massive amount of hair loss.

Even though these health conditions are deadly, the chance of infertility and kidney failure was the scariest to hear. The possibility of never being able to create a family of my own because I was selfish enough to put what other people thought of me before my own self-care crushed me. But most of all, kidney failure - my great grandfather died of kidney failure when I was eight years old and, to this day, I am able to replay the pain and distress my family encountered when he passed. I walked out of my first therapy session feeling on top of the world. I was ready to be in control of my life, rather than surrendering my power to the voice in my head telling me to not eat my favorite pizza, or to not drink my favorite frappe from Starbucks because the calorie value exceeds 100.

My journey to recovery was brutal, but definitely conquerable. There were days that I viewed my body as atrocious and refused to consume a meal. There were days I wanted to throw up the apple I ate because I saw myself as worthless. There were days my social media feed was filled with petite supermodels that were constructed of photoshop and plastic surgery, but I still wanted to unrealistically look like them.

With the endless amount of thoughts rambling in my head, I knew that the thousands of dollars my family sacrificed for therapy and a nutritionist was much more salient than the urge to not keep down my meals. I took my journey to recovery one step at a time, one meal at a time, one moment at a time and one apple at a time. I just focused on the big picture which was that I wanted to live a full and happy life. I would picture the wonderful family that I wanted to have; a healthy body that I treated well etc. With time, effort, and an amazing support system, I regained control of my life and body.

There were times that I was tempted to compare myself with people on TV, social media or otherwise but I reminded myself to be grateful for the hand I was dealt. I don't know what battle they are going through. Not everything is as it seems. I remind myself that my health is the most important thing and I continue on my journey of self-love one day at a time.

Transformation Tip

To the person reading this: distorted eating or not, your self-worth is so much more meaningful then the number displayed on the scale. It is so much more significant than the number of your pant size and the number of calories traced in a dieting app on your smartphone. Life is not about determining your lowest weight and constantly comparing yourself to those around you. From my battle, I've learned to accept that I simply cannot please everyone - they are entitled to their own opinions and preferences. And that's okay. No matter what your appearance is, your self-worth is not determined by society's expectations. You are uniquely and wonderfully made.

I learned that my core problem was not my eating disorder; my eating disorder was symptomatic of my core problem. My core problem was a self-worth problem. I fell into the trap of my eating disorder because I placed my self-worth in all the wrong things - people's compliments, my appearance, the number on the scale or trying to look "perfect". Too often people place their self-worth on their profession, their income, their appearance, etc. These things are subject to change and your self-worth should not be. You are inherently valuable as a human being. You don't have anything to prove to anyone. Stand tall in who you were created to be.

Lastly, while I was battling my disorder, my worst fear was that my habits would be discovered, and that people would intervene. Now that I am on the other side of it, I realize that I feared the one thing that could help me. Darkness and self-destructive behaviors thrive in secrecy and hide behind guilt and shame. When you confess your struggle and bring it to light, it loses its grip over you.

***If you suspect that you are struggling with an eating disorder, tell someone you trust and who you know wants the best for you. You will thank yourself later.

Devyn Faz recently graduated from high school. She has been dancing since she was two years old and dancing competitively for fifteen years. While in high school, she was actively involved in game squad and competition varsity pep. In her free time, she enjoys making memories with her friends and family. Devyn will be furthering her education at Cal State University, Fresno, in hopes to become a Physician's Assistant. For any questions or concerns, her contact email is: Devynfaz25@gmail.com

A Bad Pitch

By Bob Shield

"Difficult roads often lead to beautiful destinations"

— Zig Ziglar

Occasionally, a person gets thrown a bad pitch that they weren't expecting. In my case, it started with the infamous "reorganization" that companies do to "bring in fresh blood and start in a new direction".

I suspect it has more to do with my strong personality and the fact that I worked for an individual who needed a scapegoat whenever anything went wrong. In any event, I was called in and told of the company's new "direction" then handed a severance package.

After a bustling 38-year career, I was suddenly unemployed and unable to work without violating the terms of my severance package. I was officially in early retirement but not due to my planning or because I was ready.

Before you think this is another story about battling back from an unfair firing, think again. This was indeed a bad pitch but not the bad hop that completely changed my life. Instead, this story is about an always healthy 61-year-old suddenly being diagnosed with Prostate Cancer and how one

Chapter 2: Ultimate Survival

defining moment - the moment I received the results of a blood test- forced me to reevaluate the entirety of my life.

This story really begins after my firing when I set out on my yearly pilgrimage to get my annual checkups done. You know, schedule a trip to the General Practitioner (GP), make sure the semi-annual teeth cleaning and tooth exam is done and schedule a visit with the eye doctor for the annual exam that always ends up with the same prescription and no real change.

In the past, I had always received the call from the GP's office with rave reviews about my low bad cholesterol, my high good cholesterol, no sign of any lurking issues (diabetes and such) and their advice to keep doing whatever I was doing. I was on absolutely no medications thanks to a relatively healthy lifestyle and *really* good genes.

The call had become so routine that my trips to my GP slipped and for the last few years he didn't even order blood work for me - and I didn't insist upon him doing so. That was terrible judgement (as my wife likes to point out); we are all responsible for making sure that we get the right health care.

I missed the call from my GP's office as I was on my way to the eye doctor a few days after my blood work. The message they left was a little different than past years. All the cholesterol and such was fantastic, but the message said that they wanted to talk about the results of one specific test. It was the dreaded call that no one wants to receive because it can never be good. This particular call required that I trade phone calls with the Physician's Assistant (PA) for several hours.

When we did speak, she explained that while I got all the fantastic results that I had become accustomed to, my PSA's (Prostate Specific Antigens) were high. How high? The PA explained that anything 4 or above sends up caution flags and, in the past, mine had never exceeded 2.5. So, how high were these? 14!

This must be a big mistake. Perhaps the people drawing the blood simply made an error.

But I had a strange feeling that there was no mistake and that I would need to pursue this one carefully and quickly.

Since my formerly excellent health never required that I have a Urologist, I asked the PA to recommend one and she did. I immediately called the Urologist's office to ask for an appointment.

"Nothing available for 60 days? "

"Would it be available if I had PSA's of 14?"

"As a matter of fact, yes, we can see you next week."

Be persistent and be your own advocate. The possibility that I had any cancer *terrified* me. I knew almost nothing about the prostate or prostate cancer and, while the internet is a wonderful thing, it is also a scary place to visit when you know nothing about a topic. Some of what is out there can be frightening and much of it does not apply to your specific situation.

My wife is a melanoma survivor, and we went through her three frightening incidents with melanoma together - but women and men are vastly different. While she faced the dreaded "C" with courage and a single-minded goal of getting rid of IT, I started thinking of ways that this thing was either a mistake, something that could be handled with a pill or two, or a cruel trick.

Most men I know share an important trait with me; when it comes to their health, they are big babies that would rather hide their head in the sand and ignore a problem if left to their own devices. My wife is my rock and helped to gently keep me optimistic while preparing me to face the worst should it come. If it weren't for my wife, this would have been a much harder journey and I would have been a basket case.

The following week, I trudged to the Urologist's office so we could get to the bottom of this crazy mistake. The doctor was very professional, completely non-committal and ready to give me a thorough exam (lots of fun). If you have never had a rectal probe, I highly recommend that you cancel your next Mexican vacation and instead invite another grown man to give you a thorough rectal exam. You will never be the same again.

The doctor confirmed that my prostate was rather large; he estimated that it was twice the size of a normal walnut sized organ but insisted that was not strange for a man my age. Apparently, prostates, like my ears and nose, continue to grow as we get older making sure we cast the right profile when viewed from the side. Like any good, careful doctor he said we should let things calm down a bit and then retake the PSA test. It is possible that the body is fighting an infection or some other nefarious creature within you that has nothing to do with cancer. Good to know. So, off I went to wait five weeks to retake the test to see if things would settle down.

Of course, I also left with a new diet and an admonishment that my drinking habits needed re-evaluation and curtailment. Lots of antioxidants were to be added to my diet including blueberries and pomegranates. I was also instructed to resume drinking coffee with caffeine (I had quit many years ago because I was drinking too much) and to take a Centrum Silver and a baby aspirin daily. All that and a worrisome wait.

When the five-week mark approached, I made an appointment with my GP to talk and get my blood work done. That one conversation opened my eyes to the real likelihood that I had cancer. While reassuring and optimistic that a cure was likely, my GP was realistic and frank. PSA's of 14 are not common nor generally caused by infection or having an orgasm within 24 hours of a blood test.

And, while my Urologist didn't show his hand in what he thought of my "rectal probe", my GP made it clear that most tumors can't be felt and, even if they could, a doctor can only feel about 30% of a prostate through that means. I left knowing that, if my PSA's didn't drop dramatically, a biopsy was in my future.

The next day, I got the call. My PSA's were no longer 14! They had moved up to 16. My heart sank and reality set in. I called and got another appointment with my Urologist, knowing full well that the next step was not one I would enjoy. I had the biopsies, the testing, and the surgery. And I get my PSA's tested every eight weeks to make sure it's all held in check.

The rest of the story can be condensed into a few terse words...

Cancer Sucks.

It changes your life. It creates uncertainty and forces reevaluations. It means that the things that you thought would never change will- and sometimes forever.

But it also means you have an opportunity to reconsider who you are, what you value, what your next move will be and how you can help others. Cancer has a way of bringing perspective, clarity and even redirection.

In my case, I decided to double down on some of my favorite charity work for Habitat for Humanity; an organization dedicated to giving people a hand up, not a handout, by supplying quality housing at an affordable price. It is a wonderful organization and one that I wish I could get everyone behind.

Just as importantly, I decided to create a blog to help men that are recently diagnosed with cancer to understand the facts about the disease and the options available to them.

My personal story is still unfolding, and I take each day as it comes. While I am not certain what the future holds, I am grateful that my current priorities reflect what I treasure most. Because of cancer, my time is spent purposefully, and I would not have it any other way.

Transformation Tip

Zig Ziglar, one of my favorite sales trainers, famously said, "Always remember that your present situation is not your final destination. The best is yet to come." To me, life is full of difficult roads, rough seas, and unpredictable circumstances. Once we have traveled these, we often find the journey well worth the effort and not as difficult as we feared when we began. That has certainly been my story as my cancer journey has strengthened relationships, created new friendships, and helped me to understand what is truly important in life. Embrace the hard seasons in life because they often bring perspective and clarity.

Born in middle America near the beginning of the Baby Boomer generation, Bob Shield has always identified himself as a hard worker and someone that had to pull himself up by his own bootstraps. A son to a man whose work ethic was off the charts, Bob attended 16 different schools before finishing High School so that his father could work in construction to provide for his family. A career Business Executive, Bob now focuses on his family and his favorite charity, Habitat For Humanity www.habitat.org - helping to provide decent housing for the less fortunate and transforming communities. Bob can be reached at 707-648-1609. Follow his cancer blog at: www.bobscanceradventure.com

---

Fantasy is Full of Adventure

By Toni Barnett

Life was busy, exciting, and full of adventure, always. These days I am a little more mindful of what I engage in when boredom sets in as a direct result of an event that has shaped my life.

As the sole parent raising two kids alone back in the day, it was an unremarkable life.

I was living in a state housing community that our government had allocated to me as a single mum. I had recently separated from my husband of four years and it seemed like a kind of normal existence for a young mum at 21, or at least what I thought was normal at the time.

As a high school drop-out, pregnant at 16, everything was moving fast, and it felt like I was standing still. One minute I was a high school student, next thing my Mum and Dad were divorcing and, even more surreal, I became a Mum. I had no idea what I was meant to be as a Mother at that age, let alone a single one.

At first, I was numbed by the events of the past four years and really didn't think much of anything. It was all about survival; I had to provide for two little ones, and I had no idea how to do that. I couldn't even boil water back in those days... surely the game would be up when the cereal box was empty! It didn't take long until that desire to 'do better' kicked in. I was determined that being a sole supporting parent living on a pension was not going to be 'our' future.

I became a student teacher, worked three jobs for four years solid and finally graduated. I was hungry and not just for food. I had to give my kids a chance for a better life and it wasn't long before I was active in the community and joined the local surf lifesaving club. In fact, I remember my daughter being two and my son was five years old. Everything centred around them and each day was a new challenge. My kids were out every day at one sporting activity or another. It was a busy life.

During this time, I was invited to join an elite group of women rowers who had their sights set on National selection and the Olympic Games. In those days, there was no day care, and I had no family to look after the kids, so they just became my shadows. They attended all my training sessions, doing their homework literally on the sidelines. It was a crazy lifestyle.

Then one day, I was with some of my buddies at the surf club and was challenged to join them on a sky diving expedition. Of course, that sounded so exciting and was at the top of my bucket list, along with bungee jumping and hang gliding. Seemed the right time just before National Selection to an elite squad of women rowers- NOT!

I had as close to a perfect life as I could have wished for. I had carefully crafted a teaching career as a Phys Ed teacher, that allowed me to be with my kids most of the time working the same hours that they were at school. Holidays were the same. We were happy, fit, healthy and had just moved into an affluent area so they could attend a good high school. It was a long way from the ghetto that we had been placed in years before.

Chapter 2: Ultimate Survival

I recall the events that led up to the day we were to jump out of that perfectly good airplane like it was yesterday. Three of my close friends would take the leap with me after a day of training. We would jump from a static line which was attached to the aircraft and would open the parachute automatically so that there is no freefall involved. The intent was to be able to fly and land the canopy myself on a solo jump. This is often used in the military. Seemed like a good plan at the time.

I had no fear that day. Our mental training as high-performance athletes taught me to be laser focused on the task at hand, nothing else entered my mind.

And so, there I stood looking down from the edge of the plane...

ONE THOUSAND, TWO THOUSAND, THREE THOUSAND, FOUR THOUSAND, FIVE THOUSAND ... GERONIMO!!!

I jumped! 4000 feet into nothing, I could fly!!!

I did everything right. I followed all the training and had paid attention to the instructor like my life depended on it. Thirteen jumpers that day and I wanted to be the first, but I was the only girl and the instructor wanted me to go last. Such rubbish. I remember thinking how unfair that was just because I was the only female.

I had not given any thought to how it would all end. I was focused on one thing only and that was the drop zone, where the cross was, and I was going to land on it even though they parked the car next to the drop zone because no one ever made it on the first jump. That was until that day when Toni decided to be the first.

As I made the descent, I recall that the ground came rushing up toward me fast. I thought that was normal but was to learn later that I landed hard and fast because there was no wind to assist. This is known as a still wind landing and you absorb the full impact of landing, almost as if the parachute didn't deploy at all.

I hit the ground and instantly snapped my right ankle. I dislocated, and spiral fractured my tibia and fibula. Most of the force I took in my thighs and, fortunately, I was able to roll almost straight away. I was lucky not to have broken both ankles; my fitness at the time saved me. I was lucky to be alive.

An operation to plate and pin my ankle back together again was the new focus followed by daily non weight bearing physiotherapy for three months. This was just the beginning.

It would be some time before I was able to process how much this event would change my life. I could no longer teach Phys Ed and faced the prospect of being caged in a classroom with 39 children every day. That was never going to be ok.

I couldn't drive for nearly a year and was restricted to the lounge chair and no activity for days, weeks and months, initially. I underwent multiple operations, over several years, to correct the one before. Still to this day, I cannot wear high heel shoes or sandals on my feet. That might seem incidental, but it impacts on the way I present to meetings for my business and the choices I make when I socialise. I choose to work from home these days and take most of my meetings in front of a screen and stream my calls.

The doctors said I should not have survived the landing. I had plenty of time to reflect on what I would do next. It was while I was in recovery after the second operation to remove the metal in my ankle that I began to accept that I could no longer be a phys ed teacher. I began looking for a way I could pivot to a new career. I knew I would need to be inventive or, as I was to learn, innovative and entrepreneurial in how I would create a new opportunity. I began to study with earnest. Self-education became my "go to" and I was obsessive about how to expand my knowledge and followed a myriad of influencers and mentors over years.

There would be another three operations to rehabilitate over the years. My rowing career ended abruptly, and I became a sports administrator and reinvented a new lifestyle managing sports events and athletes.

At the end of a major event that I was working on as Media Liaison, I was offered a permanent role as a Public Relations Consultant and my new career was born. Like motherhood and teaching, I knew nothing about this new thing, but I could learn! "What's not to know?" I thought.

The parachute event was a *defining moment* for me because it has defined my pathway to become an entrepreneur. The confident leap from an airplane has played out again and again throughout my career. The truth is that I was an average athlete but I have repurposed my skills and expertise and become resourceful in applying that knowledge to a career that now provides coaching and mentoring services to women just like me to become more.

I have reflected on that time over the years and often wondered about my rowing and sports career and where I would have been today had I not taken that jump.

But here's the magic- I regret nothing. I can draw strength in times of challenge from that moment when my world shattered under that parachute.

I am often asked when I share this story, "Would you jump again?"

My answer is, "Yes, without hesitation even when I am told I would likely suffer severe injuries to my spine if I were to do it again."

However, at some point we all need to grow up and take responsibility for our lives so what I did do ten years later for my 40th birthday was to make that leap once again on the end of a bungee cord. It was exhilarating and once again I got to honour Geronimo in full voice.

I hear many of my colleagues refer to that parachuting moment as you take that leap into your next big thing in life and I close my eyes and relive that jump all over again. Today, I feel invincible like nothing can stop me. I do things without or despite fear because the alternative of not doing them is too mundane, too normal to settle for. I live my life from one exciting adventure to another still today.

I was given a second chance at life on that day and I have replayed that very scenario again and again throughout my days. I have so much more living to do and, when it becomes a little much, I take a breath and tell myself these motivating words...

When reality becomes a bore, fantasy is full of adventure.

In the words of Brene Brown, "Be brave, be courageous and step in and confidence will find you. You just have to jump!"

Transformation Tip

Don't be afraid to take the leap into new opportunities. When I experienced the parachuting accident, I could have easily allowed that bad experience to convince me that living boldly is "too dangerous" or "not worth the risk". Yes, living boldly can open you up to risk and the judgement of others but living safe at the expense of experiences, is not living at all.

When you are great at anything, you will attract both positive and negative attention from others but the only way to truly make a mark on this world is to resist holding back when your deepest desire is to pursue an opportunity. Follow your dreams! Even if things don't go according to plan, there is always a lesson and knowledge to be acquired that will aid you in your future success. Live boldly!

Toni Barnett *is a certified life and business coach. She lives and works between Perth, Western Australia, and Bali, Indonesia. A solopreneur since her early twenties, Toni founded Corporate Focus; a sports marketing and event management business that partnered not-for-profit sports organizations with corporate sponsors.*

Today, she empowers working mums who are juggling life, kids, and relationships, challenging them to step out and craft an abundant lifestyle that better meets their needs and gives them freedom to choose. She also coaches executive women in leadership inside her coaching programs. To contact Toni, email her at info@StrategicPearls.com

> *"All good things start with family."*
>
> — Toni Barnett

The Power of Prayer
By Denard Fobbs

During the time my son was deployed to Iraq, I was given the news that I had lymphoma. I had a whole family praying for my son, but I didn't tell a soul about my diagnosis, not even my wife. Instead, I decided to focus on my son.

My methodology was to say *no* to fear and to take the things I had learned about God and put them into practice. I had spent 15 years in bible study and knew what God's Word promised but had never fully put it to the test. *I decided that I would apply myself to a close and passionate pursuing of God's face in a way I had never done before.*

I asked God to protect my son and my son's platoon while he was deployed. I told God that I would stay in His face, His presence, and would trust Him by developing a daily relationship with Him. I did this through daily meditation – one hour in the morning and one hour in the evening. In the beginning, it was hard to sit still and do what God wanted me to do: to abide in Him and have a loving and close relationship that was both time-intensive and focus-intensive.

I bargained with God and told Him that I would give Him that much time every day to be in quiet reflection and relationship with Him--if he would keep my son safe. *I had to learn to shut up and simply stay in the environment.* That was where I could find and hear what He wanted me to hear.

I had a background in meditation, going back to college, but it still took effort to make the time. As a doctor, it was extremely easy for me to say I didn't have the time. *Satan will keep us busy with many distractions, as he does not want us to give God that time.*

I had (or thought I had) a contract with God. I agreed to spend this time with Him, and He agreed to protect my son. God gave us the instruction of obedience to Him, but we often forget to follow it. *God doesn't negotiate contracts with us. He demands obedience from us, but He is faithful.*

After doing that for a while, God reminded me to be open to other things, like angels surrounding my son's platoon. *God is limitless.* I visualized a host of angels keeping him and all who served with him--*safe*. My son served our country for over six years. God returned my son, safe and whole. This was an answer to my prayers.

At first, I was only praying for my son. Isn't that what we do- we limit God? We have these small brains that forget that God is GOD, and we are not. I put my son first, even ahead of my own cancer, for years. When he returned safely, I found myself not keeping my end of the bargain of closely spending time with God. There was no longer an urgent need to pray for my son's protection. I had never spent that kind of time praying for/or protecting myself.

I ended up in the emergency room. As a doctor that is a hard thing to admit. Doctors are human first. I had ignored my own health for years, knowing I had cancer, but living in denial. The tumor was about the size of a softball at that time.

My wife and family were very disturbed with the news, especially since I had not said anything to anyone for years. I went through several treatments of chemotherapy, which helped to shrink the tumor slightly, but it was still not good news. At this point, I still had stage 4 cancer.

My doctors recommended that I have a stem-cell transplant which would replace my stem cells in hopes of rescuing my bone marrow after a round of massive additional chemotherapy. During this consultation, God literally spoke to me very clearly. He told me that I didn't need the transplant, that I could go back to the same method of dwelling, living, and abiding in Him (as I had gone through with my son) – and I would be healed. This time it was for me, not my son. I knew it was God because I had never heard that voice before. I could hear Him on the inside, not audibly from the outside. It comes from the bone outward as opposed to the outside hitting your ear. When this happens, you just know- to the bone and from the heart. The peace that comes from that is overwhelming and immediate.

I told my doctors that I would not be going that route. I told them that I was going to pray for myself the same way I had prayed for my son's safety and I would get PET scans every four to six months as usually recommended.

I went back to my prayer life (the doctors thought I was nuts). The first CT PET scan showed the tumor had broken up into little pieces; it was as if someone had smashed it to 75 pieces with a hammer! When I returned for a second scan, four months later, it was completely gone.

God completely healed me.

For anyone going through similar circumstances, I would first tell them to pray and communicate with God. God directly informed most of what I did. The second thing I would share is that daily prayer is something that anyone can do. It costs nothing. It's just a commitment to get close to God and build that relationship.

God wants to heal us, and He has the power to do so. We must put ourselves in a place to allow that to work. In this sense, it's different than praying for one thing or another. It's a consistent and steadfast prayer life where we are in closeness with God-as a lifestyle. God loves us and cares about the things that concern us because we are his children. He wants to heal us. He wants to give us all that He has.

> ⁵ *But he was pierced for our transgressions,*
> *he was crushed for our iniquities;*
> *the punishment that brought us peace was on him,*
> *and by his wounds we are healed.*
>
> — Isaiah 53:5 (NIV)

> *But we all, with unveiled face, beholding as in a mirror,*
> *the glory of the Lord, are being transformed into the same image,*
> *from glory to glory, just as by the Spirit of the Lord.*
>
> — 2 Cor. 3:18

Transformation Tip

Communicate with God through prayer and meditation. Speak to Him openly and honestly. Ask questions while in prayer. Allow God to speak to you. It might take a while to recognize or hear His voice and it might even feel awkward at first. Keep pressing on. Pretty soon, it will be like second nature to you if you commit to spending time consistently with God in prayer and meditation--as a lifestyle. A consistent prayer-life will result in greater peace, joy, wisdom, and wholeness.

Dr. Denard Fobbs *practices special integrative gynecology in Fresno, California. He is finalizing a book that teaches the techniques of faith-based healing. Dr. Fobbs offers prayer and meditation techniques for patients who choose faith-based healing. Visit* www.DrFobbs.com

Chapter 2: Ultimate Survival

In Case Tomorrow Never Comes

By CaSandra Smith

It's 8 pm, the night before my major heart surgery. The cardiologist performing the surgery has just left my room after explaining tomorrow's plan and obtaining my signature to validate my understanding of all he has said.

The heart surgery I will undergo is called the TAVR; a relatively new type of aortic heart valve replacement surgery. TARV has only been around since 2004 and in the US since 2011. Though they have had great success with this type of replacement surgery, there have been times that they have had to perform open heart surgery because the heart fails to accept the new valve. If that should happen, there will be another surgeon ready to take over immediately. In the observation rooms, a kidney surgeon will be on hand to begin inserting the tubing so I can be put on dialysis after surgery should my kidneys fail during the surgery. There will also be a pulmonary surgeon should my lung fail and need to be removed. I have been told by the other cardiac surgeon that it is likely that I will not survive should I need him to perform open heart surgery if this other surgery fails.

As I lay resting the night before what could very well be my last day on earth, I look around the room. My youngest child and my sister have just left after coming to visit me. I ask myself, "Did I say everything I wanted to say to my sweet son without causing him fear?" A million other thoughts begin to hit me too. Then I remember many people are praying for me, so I delve into my faith and my panic subsides. Suddenly, I feel a calm peace.

I had been sent home during a third round of chemotherapy four years earlier having been told that there was no way to continue cancer treatment and keep me alive. I was told that I had very little time left and might only make it to the year's holiday season.

I was put into hospice care and given all the "comforts" to help me through to the end. Yet, I find myself facing this new obstacle four years later, recalling how I miraculously went into partial remission from that stage 4 lymphoma cancer. My past victory left my kidneys in a stage 4 battle, my liver with 1/3 removed, no gall bladder and no pancreas (both had been removed). My bladder function, lung function, and heart function were all left in very poor condition.

Years prior, I battled valley fever meningitis. Back in 1985, that was not something others were known to be cured from. In fact, I was one of only three patients to survive. Our survival helped the medical society produce better preventive care for patients of valley fever in today's times.

Following this, I survived 9 heart attacks and received two stents for blockages in the heart. My left lung has scar tissue in the bottom lobe making it difficult to breath and I have been on full-time oxygen for over 8 years. Prior to this last cancer, I had my thyroid removed due to thyroid cancer and a full hysterectomy because of uterine, ovarian, and cervical cancer. I have spent many hours in chemotherapy, radiation, or both, to treat these cancers. All these years of health issues have taken me here to this point.

Several days ago, the medical professionals were going to let me go home and come back in a few weeks. They wanted me to get my strength up, to face this surgery under better conditions because that would make it less concerning.

To do this, I needed to be off the IV's, catheter, heart monitor, and bi-pap machine that supports my lungs right now, along with the oxygen. So, they took me off the catheter first. I currently have an IV in my forearm on the right side, and an IV in my upper left arm as well (they are giving me two different medications that cannot travel in the same veins). On the right side, they have been adding other medications through that IV. On the left, when the medication bag is emptied in between the next dose, they have me on fluids to help support the flushing of these medicines through my kidneys.

They took me off these IV's but left the hub in my arms- just in case. Within the first hour as I was laying down, I heard "code blue, room 5036, heart hospital, code blue..". As it repeats, I'm thinking to add prayer for that patient. As nurses and doctors are in my room putting me back on these IV's, I wonder *why aren't they trying to help the code blue patient?* Then I realize... I'm the code blue patient! I laughed in my mind. (I was not awake to them). That was when they, and I knew, I was not leaving the hospital. That was 4 days ago, but the days seem to be running into each other; a byproduct of my long stay at the hospital.

This brings me to my next point - while days can be similar, no two days are the same. I think that is how life is meant to be: while we can plan, we are not supposed to know *exactly* what the day will bring. Instead, we should appreciate the distinctiveness of each day and live it as if it were our last. We should appreciate all that the day brought so that, if we never see tomorrow, we can go, satisfied knowing that the culmination of our life was enough.

Should tomorrow be my last day, I have given and received enough.

I have never felt that I understood my life purpose enough to label it, but if I were to label it tonight it would be to spread His message of joy through loving others. Should I live beyond this surgery, I will just have more people to meet and love, teaching them to find joy, as we have been promised. My love, like His (my creator) is real for everyone I encounter and even those I have never met personally.

As I mentally prepare for tomorrow's surgery, I wonder, have I lived my life long enough and *well* enough? Do my children know what they need to in order to have good lives? I do know that none of us know when it is our time to leave this earth.

I've had people hear about my illnesses in life and, with all their wisdom, suggest that perhaps It occurred because I am suppressing negative emotions and if I release those emotions, my mind will be less stressed and my body can heal. Come on, how ridiculous is this?! If this were true, how do they explain birth defects? They obviously just don't understand.

I understand that a person will live a freer existence if they don't harbor ill will from the past. I believe in the power of both positive thought and energy and know that you cannot reach your highest potential if you constantly bombard your mind with past negatives. So, letting go of the past is important- when done the right way. We should not dwell on the past but, instead, work through negative feelings and release them to heal.

As I sit here in anticipation for my surgery tomorrow, I ruminate on all the sweet lessons that life has gifted me. I believe that we can all learn from the life lessons of another so I would like to share what life has taught me. Like sifting through items at a garage sale, take ownership of what you deem worthy and bypass what you feel is not for you.

This is what I know...

I am, and have been, only one of my children's teachers on earth, and I have also been a student of theirs in many ways. I trust that my children have been given enough by me. In my humanity, I am sure that there are things I have overlooked but I believe that they will learn everything they need in life. I have provided them with the right places to gain the right things that they may or may not choose to have for their lives, so I have no regrets. If you are a parent, do not underestimate the power of positioning your children so they are exposed to the valuable things that you may not be able to teach them. It takes a village so build yours wisely.

I've lived a good life. I've been to many places in this world. I have always known somehow that the Lord promises us riches. He gave us this whole earth from birth. We can choose to see all of it, or only parts of it. I sometimes think about all the natural resources on this wonderful planet that have been made available for our betterment such as gold, water, food and minerals. While we should respect and conserve these precious resources, I appreciate that they are available to us. Likewise, be grateful for the abundance made available to you simply because you live on this glorious planet.

And oh how we are unique and magnificent as a species! We are social and rational beings. We are both innovative and creative with the ability to produce ideas that can better our lives and the lives of others. Our ideas can afford us the capacity to live a quality life. Yes, the Lord wants us to have riches. I am grateful for the knowledge and unwavering faith that I possess. Never take for granted the fact that we were built to be a wellspring of wisdom and knowledge. Don't let your well dry up. Always seek to evolve and self-actualize.

I believe that everyone that I have met in this life are exceptional. Whether they are family, friends, or not friends yet, I know that each relationship played a role in my evolution as a person. Simply knowing each person was a gift. Regardless of the amount of moments, quality of those moments and length of time our lives attached, I am truly grateful. Every experience comes with a lesson- even the painful ones. So, while we may feel regret in moments, embrace every part of our story recognizing that diamonds are made in the fire.

Just like I was thinking over the material wealth in our earth, I recognize that the Lord provides us with people to bless us and give us exactly what we need. Sometimes I have been at the right place, right time, and the right circumstance puts a person or people around that help without plan to give me what I need. Sometimes also, I have known to ask. Which brings me to my next nugget of wisdom: Never think that you cannot ask for help whether you are asking for directions, a recommendation, a jump for your car or an extra set of hands on moving day, ask away! Closed mouths don't get fed.

This concludes my love letter to you with the exception of my last and perhaps most important piece of advice which can be found in the following transition tip…

Transformation Tip

Ask yourself the following question:

If I knew my days were numbered and I only had X amount of days to live (you fill in the blank), would I change where I invest my time, energy and money?

If the answer is YES, consider the following piece of advice:

Don't wait until you are faced with the urgent possibility of death to prioritize the things that you will value at the end of your life. Instead, recognize the inevitable truth that your days are already numbered. You are one day closer to death with each day you live. While that may sound morbid, let it excite you because it is a pressing reason to live an intentional life!

While there is wisdom in having discipline and doing things you don't always enjoy in order to build a better future, preparation for the future should never lead us to completely neglect the things we truly value in life. There is nothing worse than being at the end of your life and realizing that you spent all your time investing in and focusing on the wrong things.

I challenge you to make a list of the things you value (the things that really set your soul on fire, your relationships with the most precious people in your life etc.) and come up with a life plan that allows you to attain your goals while still nourishing these things. You won't regret it.

CaSandra Smith *is a woman who has delved into living her life to the fullest starting with early careers in music, then as a businesswoman and speaker/trainer. She now lives in Arizona and trains companies to build strong customer relationships with their clients. She is grateful to have hit all of her bucket list items. She focuses on kindness to others, sharing love and the joy of living. She can be reached at heartcards4u@gmail.com or follow her on Facebook: https://www.facebook.com/j.casandra.smith*

3

Turning Your Vice Into Your Victory

In Memory of Amy Wall

By Joe Avila

Just a mile from my home on the side of the freeway there is a sign that reads: "Please don't drink and drive" and a smaller sign beneath it reads: "In memory of Amy Wall". Amy Wall is the seventeen-year-old girl who I killed while driving on the freeway drunk in 1992. A fatal consequence to my life of drinking alcohol and drug use.

I grew up in a small town in Fresno County, California, where it was not unusual for teenagers to drink alcohol and roust about town. It was no secret that there would be little to no discipline should we get caught drinking by the local constable or school official. The lax disciplinary measures combined with the thrill chasing of youth were the perfect recipe for a life where alcohol took center stage.

As I grew into adulthood, I frequented bars and made up any excuse to party. Alcohol was always present. I worked hard so I could play hard. I really don't remember a day where alcohol wasn't present in some form and partying frequently had bad results. I had several "Driving Under the Influence of Alcohol" citations and spent several nights in jail, but never really did any long period behind bars. My drinking caused several accidents in my life and I am paying the price now, with limited use of my back, shoulder, and legs. I live with a lot of pain

That night in 1992, I was arrested for Vehicular Manslaughter and Driving Under the Influence of Alcohol. My bail was set at one million dollars, so I had to prepare to spend a lot of time in jail. During the first five days after my crime, I was looking for an opportunity to kill myself. I was ashamed, angry, and felt incredibly sorry for what I had done. Because I was being observed closely by jail staff, I couldn't find an opportunity.

So, on that fifth day, my neighbor asked a chaplain if he would come see me. He took me out of my cell and escorted me to a small office where we talked for several hours. He then told me something that changed my life forever. He said, "Joe, Jesus Christ died on the cross even for what you did five days ago." This was a *defining moment* for me because it was in this moment that I decided to ask the Lord Jesus Christ into my life. This decision has changed my life forever.

About two months later, I appealed to the courts to lower my bail and succeeded. My bail was lowered so I could post bail on one condition: that I would commit myself to a rehabilitation facility to deal with my alcoholism. All the "twenty-eight day" programs in the area were full and my last chance to get into a facility was the Salvation Army six-month program.

I enrolled in the program and committed to do my best to deal with my drinking problem. I also committed to search the Scriptures and apply everything I learned in the Bible to my life. God was changing me and preparing me for what was to come. I fell in love with my Savior Jesus Christ and laid all my troubles at His feet.

In 1992 I had been married for twelve years and had two beautiful daughters. Our marriage was not perfect, yet we loved each other and made it through some pretty bad times. I believe without this strong bond we would not have made it through what was about to come.

While I was in the Salvation Army, I continued with my court appearances and trying to get the charges against me lowered. At the same time, through my Bible studies and life-changing counseling and classes, God was changing me. I was willing to accept responsibility for all of my sins and knew God had forgiven me for all my wrongs, even the one I did on that September night.

After considering what my victim's family was going through, my wife and I decided to change my plea and put an end to the painful court proceedings. We called our lawyer and told her to inform the court. She cautioned us that there were no deals on the table, and I was setting myself up to receive a very stiff sentence. She was right.

While in jail, Ron Claassen and Elaine Enns visited me. They were from The Center for Restorative Justice and Peace Making at Fresno Pacific University. Ron and Elaine counselled me and taught me about the "Miracle of Reconciliation". They taught me the principles of reconciliation and restoration. I learned that God had forgiven me for my wrongs and how to forgive myself. They shared how the road to reconciliation is an exceedingly difficult one that begins with those closest to you. I remember when I asked my wife for forgiveness and then my children. I continued to seek forgiveness from so many I had hurt over the years. In some cases, I don't know if they really forgave me.

I understood that I had to be a changed person and truly walking with God in order to seek forgiveness in a way that truly honored those I had hurt. Ultimately, my dream was to someday reconcile with my victim's friends and family. That possibility would be years away.

On the day I was to appear in court to change my plea, my wife and I arrived at the courthouse early. While on the courtyard grounds, we committed our marriage to be a triune one: a marriage between her, myself, and Jesus Christ. We promised each other to always invite Christ into the middle of what decisions we had to make and to rely on Him for all the answers in our life.

We made it to the courtroom, and it was filled with Amy's family and friends as well as mine, each group on their own side of the courtroom. This is when I realized I had driven a wedge between my family and friends and Amy's.

On both sides of the courtroom sat great people who would probably embrace each other at a different time in their life. This crime did not just affect a few people, it affected a whole community and I had to live with what I had done.

The proceedings were very short. I told the judge that I wanted to change my plea to "guilty" on all charges then I was immediately remanded back into custody. The date for my sentencing was set and a request for an evaluation from the probation department was requested. I would be sentenced on the day after Easter 1993.

The day for sentencing came quickly and I was prepared for a prison sentence; I just didn't know how long. The day of sentencing was a difficult one for Amy's and my family. The judge had received the probation report and they were recommending the maximum sentence. My prior offenses were also weighing on the Judge's mind. Amy's family and friends shared about their relationship with Amy. My friends and family shared about their relationship with me. It was very difficult listening to how precious of a person Amy was and equally difficult to hear from my family.

I was able to address Amy's family and tell them how sorry I was for taking Amy from them. Finally, it was up to the Judge to have the last word. He told me that I was an alcoholic and that I probably would never change. He said he was doing everything in his power to make sure I would not hurt anyone again. He gave me the maximum sentence he was allowed by law: twelve years in the California State Penitentiary. I was taken from the courtroom and went back to the jail to prepare to be transported to a prison in California.

While in prison, I continued to study the Bible and took as many classes as I could to strengthen my walk with Jesus. I attended Patten University while incarcerated and received a correspondence scholarship through Bethany Bible College in Alabama.

My time in prison was also spent working in the hospital and ministering to those prisoners in Hospice Care. I really loved praying with those who were about to leave this world yet giving them assurance of the glory they were about to see. I was also involved with the chapel and managed a peer counseling program where we had twelve active groups meeting every week.

On January 3, 1999, I was released from prison and able to go home to be with my family. That evening friends and relatives came to welcome me home. My eldest daughter brought her friends over to meet me. Even though I had spent six years in prison, she was proud of the person I had become and wanted to share me with her friends.

The next few weeks would be fast and crazy: clothes shopping, DMV and Social Security office visits and relearning many things and getting acquainted with the internet. The most important meeting within the first few days of my release was with the director of the local office of Prison Fellowship Ministries: Austin Morgan. Austin offered me a part time job and a laptop computer. I needed to learn how to use the computer knowing that it would be a very big part of my future. I continued volunteering for Prison Fellowship Ministries after my part time job had ended.

The first weekend home I joined my wife and children at New Hope Community Church for Sunday services. The pastor there had been preparing the congregation for my homecoming. When we arrived at the church, all the trees were wrapped with yellow ribbons and there was a banner over the front door that read "Welcome Home Joe". I knew that moment this was my home church and it still is to this day.

On January 3, 2000, a year after my release from prison to the day, I went to work for Prison Fellowship Ministries. I have just celebrated my twentieth year with this amazing ministry. I have traveled to hundreds of prisons and reached out to thousands of prisoners, ex-prisoners, and their families. I share the "Good News" with all of them so that they can have a life-saving relationship with Jesus Christ as I do.

The Rest of the Story

A few years after my release from prison and well into my work with Prison Fellowship and the community, our Police Chief asked if I would go on the radio with him to promote a first time DUI class he was starting. I accepted his invitation and while on the radio Amy's brother and father were listening to the show.

The next day I received a call from my mentor Ron Claassen. He had just gotten off the phone with Derek, Amy's brother. Derek wanted to meet with me; Ron and his wife would be our mediators.

The miracle Ron and Elaine told me about years ago was about to come true. Derek, his pastor, my wife, and I met with Ron and his wife on an evening at the Fresno Pacific University campus. We prayed at the start and introductions and rules were given for the meeting.

Derek started the dialogue and told me how much Amy meant to him. She was his older sister. He told me about the great times they had together and how he hated me for what I had done ten years earlier. He also told me that he had wished that I had gotten the electric chair for what I had done. I was able to tell him about the life I had lived as an alcoholic and how sorry I was for taking his sister from him.

He also told me that he and his family had been watching me for many years and that they approved of how I was living my life. I asked him to forgive me for taking Amy from him and he did. He gave me a picture of Amy and said I could use it when I spoke across the country. A few months later I met with Rick, Amy's father and then Linda, Amy's mother, and I have experienced the miracle of reconciliation. I am who I am today through God's saving grace and could never experience this miracle without Him in my life.

Chapter 3: Turning Your Vice Into Your Victory

Transformation Tip

I wish this tragedy had never happened to the Wall family. It happened because I drank and drove. Please be responsible and call a friend if you drink too much. If you think you have a drinking or drug problem- tell someone. There are too many of us who care for you and want to see you be well.

Joe Avila is the National Director for Angel Tree Sports Clinic and Special Events at Prison Fellowship Ministries. Joe is an ordained minister and received his education from Patten Bible College, Oakland CA and Bethany Bible College, Dothan Alabama. He has served on the Board of Elders for his church and is on the Board of Directors for the Victim Offender Reconciliation Program (VORP), Circles of Support and Accountability (COSA), founded First Base After-Care Ministry, helped found Welcome Home Ministries of the Central Valley. Joe also serves on the State of California Department of Corrections Volunteer Advisory Task Force and is a special consultant to several state legislators. Joe is the founder of Angel Tree Sports Clinic for Prison Fellowship Ministries

Joe has been with Prison Fellowship for 20 years and resides in Fresno, CA with his wife Mary. They are blessed with two daughters, Elizabeth who resides in La Jolla, CA with her husband Brian, and Grace who lives in Texas with her husband, Mark. Joe spends as much of his spare time as possible traveling between Southern California and Texas to see and spoil his three granddaughters, Emma, Violet and Rosemary. For more info on the Prison Fellowship program visit: www.prisonfellowship.org

Don't Hide the Scars

By Flindt Andersen

On September 9, 1955, my parents never imagined that I would grow up to be a drug addict. You see, that was the day I was born and even though I didn't know it, I was born with a birth defect that would have an everlasting effect on my life. The first few days of my life were filled with multiple surgeries and hospital stays. As the years went on, I was required to have at least one surgery per year until the age of 13. Of course, I had no idea that the opioid medications they had been giving me all those years had already taken hold of those receptors in my brain and the storm was about to hit.

I actually got a break from those surgeries from 13 to 18 years of age but during my junior high and high school years I was always experimenting with different substances to hide the emotional and physical pain I had gone through. My awareness of the fact that I was going to have to endure more physical pain as I got older wore on me and the drugs helped me cope. Although I was a good student, good athlete, and a musician, my secret life was always kept under wraps.

As the years went on through college, marriage and raising a family, my addiction skyrocketed to levels that would have killed most people. The surgeries continued and the amount of both prescription drugs from the doctors and the illegal ones I was taking would have put down a herd of elephants. To this day, it's hard to believe that I am still walking around.

From 1980 to 2001, I had a heart attack, open heart bypass surgery, femoral artery surgery, knee and back surgeries and of course the famous rectal surgery because I had taken so many narcotics that it was almost impossible to have a bowel movement. In fact, I tore my insides up so bad they had to go in to repair that. Trust me, that's no fun. I literally led a double life. I owned my own business and was fortunate to have people that worked for me because my job everyday was to make sure I had enough pills to take so I wouldn't get what we call "Dope Sick".

Addiction to pain killers like Vicodin, Norco, Oxycodone, Oxycontin and a variety of other opioids build up a tolerance in one's body. Consequently, the number of pills I took each day in order to function increased over the years. At least I thought I was functioning. During these years, it was all one big lie! I lied to my family, friends, co-workers but especially to all the doctors I was seeing. I even made up fake injuries so I could get more drugs. It was a constant battle to stay one step ahead of the bill collectors, the drug dealers and all those people I had harmed along the way, and that was a very large number.

By 2001, I had a drug habit that required me to take over 70 Vicodin every day. If I had more, I would have taken more. When one is taking that many pills, they just don't fall out of the sky. I was now stealing and forging prescriptions that I would steal out of the doctor's offices. I was even caught by the DEA.

People sometimes don't believe that a person can take that many pills. That's because most people don't understand the addictive qualities of these drugs and the hold they can have on you.

In 2001, after numerous attempts at getting clean and after my heart surgery in 2000, I knew I was in a huge amount of trouble. I was 45 years old, my family despised me, my friends didn't trust me, and my business was in the toilet. I weighed 140lbs and couldn't fit in my 13 year old's jeans because I was too skinny.

My *defining moment* occurred as I was sitting in the hospital just coming out of the ICU with an intubation tube down my throat. My children walked in, took one look at me, and turned around and walked out. At that moment I knew I would lose them forever if I didn't get help!

On March 2, 2001, I stopped by my best friend's office and he decided to help me after so many people had tried and I wouldn't listen. I don't know exactly why I listened to him that day, but I did. I believe it was because I was at the point where I knew something needed to change in my life. I was tired of feeling out of control.

I entered the Betty Ford Treatment Center on March 5, 2001 and now have almost 20 years of recovery. As I write this very short story, I can only say that there is much more to this than what I have put down here.

Maybe someday I will have the time to share my story in depth. These days, I'm pretty busy though. Since getting clean and sober, I have been helping people in recovery. In 2009, I started an organization called PAIN, Parents & Addicts in Need. Since the inception of PAIN, we have seen over 3,500 families and helped over 2,000 individuals get the proper treatment they need to get clean and sober, stay that way and live good, long productive lives.

Instead of hiding my scars and past experiences, I opt to share my story so that others can learn from it and be encouraged.

My story is definitely not over, I believe it's ongoing. Nowadays, I focus on helping others to prevent them from going down the destructive road that I chose early on. Most of us will not make it back.

Transformation Tip

Do not be afraid to reach out for help if you're struggling with addiction. Be selective on who you are reaching out to; there are a lot of people who will take advantage of you. You can call our office for help. (559) 579-1551.

Flindt Andersen is the Founder & President of: PAIN, Parents & Addicts in Need (www.gotpainusa.org). PAIN helps those struggling with addiction by providing detox/residential programs and support for the families of those individuals that are in treatment. Pain was founded in 2009 and currently serves residents throughout California. In order to help create awareness on the opioid crisis and the nature of addiction, Flindt often speaks at Universities, legal forums (Bar Associations), medical groups and professional associations.

Freedom in Forgiveness

By Toni Odonnell

I always like to say I was born the year Disneyland opened, 1955. I was raised in a small mountain town with two sisters, one older, the other younger, and it seemed idyllic to me. We had plenty of space to run, climb and explore. I loved being outdoors so playing outside as a child was always a source of joy for me.

At the age of 10, reality hit. My father, who was an educator and quite demonstrative and funny, had a dark secret. He had been victimized and molested as a young boy and had turned into a victimizer. I escaped by refusing his manipulation, but my sisters were not as lucky. Although I suspected that something in my house was not right, it wasn't until I was an adult that I discovered that both had been sexually abused by him starting at the age of 10.

We moved to the city when I started 8th grade, and by the time I was in high school I had an extremely active social life, was popular and a straight A student. At a friend's invitation, I began attending Youth for Christ events. It was there, at the age of 16, that I heard about God the Father. He was kind and compassionate and desired a personal relationship with us. I longed for a Father like that, so I accepted Jesus Christ as my personal savior. The year was 1972.

I had an immediate passion for the Bible, learning everything I could which led to a burning desire in my soul to serve overseas as a missionary. It was not to be. Trying to survive in a dysfunctional family with secrets took its toll. The secret was finally revealed to me, by my little sister, that my father had been sexually abusing her from the age of 10 to 14. I, in turn, told the secret and it blew the family apart. We would not recover for years.

I began to run, which included two marriages that ended in divorce, with a son from each marriage. I began to be viewed as the "black sheep" and, by the time I was 30, I started to embrace that view. The black sheep is thought to be the most sensitive person in the family and takes on all of the energy and dynamics in the rest of the family – then reflects it back like a mirror. The black sheep often receives negative attention, but the family dysfunction emerges and he or she can become a catalyst for awareness and change.

When I looked back at my relationship with God, and all the dreams that were now shattered, the pain, shame, and guilt took over. I began to drink which helped quiet my thoughts and the voice in my head that told me I was worthless.

I met my third and current husband during this time, and for whatever reason, which I now know was a gift from God, he decided to take me on, along with my two sons. We were absolutely a broken mess. At the same time, my father who had remarried 13 years earlier, had been arrested for sexually abusing his stepdaughter. He was brought to trial and given a 24 year prison sentence. My excessive drinking was now my coping mechanism beyond self-medication. I was a full-blown alcoholic.

Over the next eight years, while committing slow suicide, I barely survived. After a particularly bad binge, I had a dream that I had died, and my sons had not one good thing left of me - nothing positive that they could say about their mother. I woke up devastated and knew I had hit my bottom.

I made a call and found a recovery program. I quickly found that this 12-step program required participants to be rigorously honest and shed the victim mentality. The underlying message of the program was service to others with God as your first and main focus. Addicts are such self-centered people, they're not even aware that their first thought is themselves. I believe Satan uses this same tactic on anyone going through a rough time or crisis.

I got sober May 5, 1999 and now have 21 years of sobriety. I can remember in the early days of recovery, one of my tricks to pray before I left the house, was to put my car keys under my bed so I would remember to get on my knees.

I made a promise to Jesus the day I quit drinking. I vowed to chase him harder than I had chased the bottle. I made a promise no matter how humiliated or how much I had to humble myself, I would never quit. I made a promise that I would never say no to anything unless I had a genuinely good reason for it. I had to begin by making amends to my family; a living amends where they could see the change. And they did.

During this time, I found a church that I could plug into, where I could be mentored and learn, or relearn the things I had forgotten about my Lord and Savior. And this began my new journey which, being extremely consistent and driven to know Jesus as my savior, led me on a path of peace, love and service to others. The biggest thing was learning how to forgive myself for how poorly I had raised my boys. Another major hurdle that I found myself facing was offering forgiveness to my father who had ruined our lives, destroyed our family, and created such wreckage and pain. It certainly wasn't easy, but it was something that had to be done if I wanted to walk in true freedom and increase my odds of staying sober.

I went to the prison where he was incarcerated and that began a journey I would never see coming. I was able to talk about my relationship with God to my dad. He started asking God to let him live to get out so he could make amends to his daughters. At the same time, my sisters both began to change their hearts from hatred and bitterness, to wanting to forgive him. They saw what forgiving him had done in my life and wanted to experience the same type of freedom that I was walking in.

My father finished his 24 years, which is a miracle for an incarcerated sex offender, was released, and is living today with regular communication with his daughters. Only God can bring about that kind of healing, as long as we are obedient to where He sends us. That is the Gospel message. Being reconciled one to another and with God.

In 2007, with so much energy, prayers and much needed work having been poured into my family, and many ministry opportunities I had led or participated in, God opened the door for me to take a mission trip to India. It was time to take the healing He had given me and share my story and offer hope to others living in spiritual darkness and poverty.

When you're helping someone work through their pain and paralysis of a stronghold, your own stumbling block turns into a steppingstone. I chose to use my story for the Glory of God.

Today, what started as a ten day short-term mission trip, has developed into a love I cannot describe. Over the years I have been given incredible opportunities to continue to work and travel to my adopted country. I have a nonprofit called, "The Least of These - India" that supports a preschool for 60 children in a slum of 20,000, an orphanage/safe house for children, and a tutoring program for 40 students. All of these children are the outcast of India - much as I felt once upon a time.

I believe, beyond a shadow of a doubt, that I would not be living the life that I am right now, if I hadn't forgiven my father. God has blessed me and made my life so rich that I have no words to describe it. At 16, God called me overseas and it wouldn't be until I was 52 that I would get the opportunity...and it would be God's perfect timing. It's never too late.

People my age love to tell me I need to slow down, take something off my plate. I have two responses.... "I'd rather burn out than rust out" and "God has not told me how big my plate is." So, until He does, I will continue to fill it with service. I'll stop when the doors close. It's not just surviving, it's thriving.

Transformation Tip

Freedom in Forgiveness

Unforgiveness is like a chain around your heart that keeps you from experiencing the freedom that God desires for you. Unforgiveness towards another person renders us a slave to them—not the other way around.

When you refuse to release the bitterness, anger, or resentment that you feel towards a person who has wronged you, you tether yourself to that person or situation.

When a worm is left to live freely in an apple, it wanders around eating away at its inside creating harmful shafts inside the core of the apple- it's heart. It literally destroys the apple from the inside! Unforgiveness has the same destructive effect on our mind, heart, and soul.

In Matthew 6:14-15 Jesus says, "For if you forgive others their trespasses, your heavenly Father will also forgive you, but if you do not forgive others their trespasses, neither will your Father forgive your trespasses."

If you want to be truly reconciled to God and free to fulfill the plans he has for you, you MUST forgive others and absolve their debt to you in the same way that God has done for all of us.

Doing so, makes you more like our heavenly Father and will cut the chain around your heart so that you are truly free to go wherever God leads you.

> *"Brothers and sisters, I do not consider myself yet to have taken hold of it. But one thing I do: Forgetting what is behind, and straining toward what is ahead, I press on towards the goal to win the prize for which God has called me heavenward in Christ Jesus."*
>
> — **Philippians 3:13-14**

In 2007, India and her people become a passion and calling for **Toni Odonnell***. She is the Founder and President of a nonprofit called "The Least of These-India" which seeks to transform lives and communities through education. The three ministries in India supported by this nonprofit are: Gregory Memorial School, Simon House and an after-school tutoring program called Ashananda Care.*

These ministries inspire children by sharing the gospel of Jesus Christ while providing tangible assistance towards academic success. Toni is passionate about studying the Word of God, and teaching and mentoring other women either in a group study or one on one. She has been sober for 21 years and continues to work in recovery. She has been married to her husband Patrick for 29 years and has two sons, two daughters-in-law and five grandchildren. Toni can be reached at tonioluke22@comcast.net

My Own Teen Challenge
By Charlie Campbell

This is a reality check. It is probably one of the most impactful *defining moments* in my life. My real father was never in the picture. The story I got was that he just left. So, from the time I was about six years old when I was adopted by my stepfather, I became very angry at my real father.

The hurt and the pain of feeling abandoned, the pain like no one wanted you. How could my real father want nothing to do with me? That thought kept ringing in my head. What did I do wrong? Where did I go wrong? All these questions could not be answered because I had no idea where he was.

My heart filled with hurt, anger and pain. My stepfather and my mother were alcoholics and I would literally watch them fight night after night. I began to live in fear and there were times I was even scared for my life.

By the time I compounded all of those circumstances together, I was 12 years old. I was a full-blown IV-using drug addict. I was using cocaine and crystal meth to numb the pain. Because of starting at such an early age, by the time I was in high school, my habit had become large...and expensive. I had no choice but to rob, steal and sell drugs to make things work out.

This led to a life of being arrested. I was in and out of rehab, in and out of jail, in and out of detoxes - just a crazy cycle that had become unmanageable. For small periods of time, I was able to hide it. I went into a marriage hiding all these things I felt inside. I had two twin children, yet this lifestyle crept back in. It became known to everyone.

At the age of 31, I finally got to meet my real father - and this is when I had the reality check. After talking to him and asking him questions like "where have you been? Why haven't you called? What about Christmas? What about birthdays?"

You know what the strangest thing was? I actually met my father selling drugs to him. He and I sat in my motel room one night. He answered these questions, but he answered them in a way that was a slap in the face.

He said, "I had a 25-year sentence that I had to go do."

Due to my addiction, he said "I want to ask you a couple of questions. When was the last time that you spoke to your children?" At that time, it had been months. He said, "When was the last time you sent them gifts?" At that time, It had been months.

He said, "There's not much difference between me and you. See, I did it to you and now you're doing it to them."

And this was my reality check. It was like a bolt of lightning went down my spine. It was that moment that I decided things had to change. After he left, I remember sitting on my bed and I just said, "God, you're going to have to stop me, cuz I cannot stop myself."

It was literally an hour or two after that I was driving down the road and was arrested with six ounces of methamphetamines. With the life that I had lived, this would have been my fifth felony, if convicted.

Eight months later, I was sitting in my cell on my bed in solitary confinement. I was all alone, just rethinking that conversation that we had had. Not only that, I had divorce papers in my hand dictating that I would never see my children again, that I was going to prison for a minimum of 125 years.

I was lost. I was scared. But I made a decision.

I stood up off my bed. I drew a line on the floor with my foot and I stepped across that line and I said, "I'm never going to live like that again. If given a chance, I'm going to be the best person I can be. I'm going to live the best life that I can live. I'm going to be the best father I can be."

As I stood in front of the judge for my 5th court appearance, things were not looking very good for my hand. The only chance I had was to get into a program called Teen Challenge.

The closing statements started, and the judge asked me a few questions.

He said, "Son, as long as you've been on drugs, the statistics say there is a 90% chance, you'll never change your life. Not only that, being that you've already been to prison twice - statistics show an 80% chance that that's where you'll spend the rest of your life. The sad thing is that there is also a 70% chance that your children are going to follow in your footsteps. Why should we give you a second chance? How do you answer these questions?"

I didn't have an answer because I had felt very hopeless, that I was a lost cause and that this was just how my life was going to be forever.

But I had Pastor Brian Wilson with me.

And he said, "Judge, those are man's statistics. But I serve a living God and with my God all things are possible. I believe God is telling us that this young man has a 10% chance that he's going to change his life. That he has a 20% chance that he is not going to go to prison. You said the great news is that when he changes his life, he changes his family history and there's a 30% chance that his children will not follow in his footsteps. Behind you on the wall, it says 'In God We Trust'. How do you answer to that?"

Then the judge agreed to give me a second chance and let me go to a Teen Challenge program. I took it as the grace of God. They taught me the information I needed to cope with my pain. They gave me tools to change my life and I applied them to my life. It has been radically changed forever.

I am forever grateful to that judge and his grace. Otherwise, my life would be very different right now.

In the time I was incarcerated the only book I had to read was the Bible. In the reading of this word, I found a process that changed my life forever that I want to share with you today. They're much like the steps of Alcoholic Anonymous, but I back them with a scripture.

Transformation Tip

If anyone knew what I needed, it would be my creator. By the promises of God who created me, these are what we call the steps to Freedom:

1. We have admitted our powerlessness.
2. Come to belief in Jesus Christ.
3. Affirm my need for the care of God.
4. Auditing my life.
5. Accounting for my actions.
6. Agreeing with God.
7. Abandoning my old life of sin.
8. Amending my ways.
9. Acting on my amends.
10. Analyzing my walk with Christ.
11. Anchoring my life with Christ.
12. Advancing my faith.

All these are backed by scripture and can be explained in more detail.

Charlie Campbell went on to become the director of that same Teen Challenge center and has spent years giving back to other troubled youth. He also helped start the first men's center in Mississippi. If you would like more information on the steps, or encouragement from someone who understands pain, you can email him at campbellcause@yahoo.com. For more info on Teen Challenge, visit: www.teenchallengeusa.org

Portraits of Hope
By Lance Pearce

I was born to a mother who chose not to keep me, and a father who did not know of me. I was raised by a mother who would try to love me, as best as she could. The two father figures I had in my life would leave me broken, in a need for approval and with an overall feeling of worthlessness. Despite their brokenness, they were my family and the only role models I had.

While growing up, I began to use alcohol and drugs to help numb my pain. However, I would soon find out that this self-medication was creating a greater problem then the pain I was trying to numb. This void I was trying to fill was unfillable. It led me to reckless and self-destructive behavior which resulted in overdosing, being arrested, and losing many close relationships.

Over the years, I quit using the various types of drugs. However, for the next 15 years, my life would still be affected by alcohol. While looking for answers I began to submerge myself into the church. I put myself through the Police Academy and got hired as a Police Officer. During all of this I realized that as long as alcohol was in my life everything was still at risk. What I had to protect were my two daughters and my new career.

I did not place enough value in my own life to quit drinking, but I valued my daughters enough to quit. For them, I had the strength. So, I decided to quit drinking cold turkey to safeguard my relationship with my children. This was a *defining moment* in my life because I now had a purpose and the motivation to become a better man for my kids and myself.

Almost as a reward for choosing sobriety, I was blessed to meet my future wife, Karen Nagata. Ironically, we met during the first night that I had gone out after becoming sober. She would stand by my side, as I submerged myself deeper into the church in order to find some way to give back and to continue my growth. The healthier I got mentally, emotionally, and physically, the more I felt I had to give to others who were hurting. I knew I wanted to help those in need but wasn't sure how I could be of service to others. I kept praying for the Lord to show me what to do so I could find and fill this calling.

Then one day I saw a homeless man standing on the corner and I felt a strong desire to speak to and pray for him. I approached him and asked if I could pray with him. He agreed to the prayer and began sharing his story. As we shared some time in fellowship, I realized that my life's path put me in a position to minister to this man and other men and women who have found themselves in a place of brokenness. This was the start of my street ministry: **Portraits of Hope**.

I now routinely go out into the streets to talk with and pray for those who are homeless and broken. Many of the people I speak to are addicted, hopeless and hurting. Most have had difficult lives, making it easier for them to slip into addiction, as I once did. I am able to be a source of encouragement and give them a platform to share their stories.

To personalize their story, I take their portrait and post their story on social media in order to raise awareness of addiction and homelessness. I offer each person a care package, water, prayer and resources. Resources to help them face their addiction and get off of the streets.

Portraits of Hope has brought so much purpose into my life. I believe God gave me this ministry so that I can share the goodness of God's grace and mercy with people who are struggling. I talk openly about my past with the people I meet, to give them hope that it is never too late to turn their life around. Mostly, I just provide a listening ear and oftentimes it is just what they needed to restore their sense of dignity and show them that they are worthy and valuable. That they matter and are not forgotten.

Transformation Tip

While growing up, I did not realize that my "Father Wounds" and "Mother Wounds" had made such an impact on my life. They made me angry, bitter, and left me with a large void. A void which I tried to numb and fill with various substances and self-destructive behaviors. However, the pain was still there and voids were unfillable.

Addiction is like a false rock of salvation to a drowning person. As they find themselves drowning in their pain, they reach out and hold onto that false rock of salvation (addiction). However, that rock will drag them to the bottom and will keep them there. That is, until they are willing to let go of that false rock of salvation (addiction), and only then will they be able to swim back up.

I now rely on the living, breathing word of Jesus Christ to fill my voids and to take my pain. To replace the anger with love and to replace bitterness with forgiveness. I am by no way fixed. For I am still broken, but I am now a work in progress.

Lance Pearce is the owner of Lance Pearce Photography www.lancepearcephotography.com and the creator of the Portraits of Hope Street Ministry www.facebook.com/portraitsofhope/

> *"Through the power of prayer, these portraits, and testimonies, I hope to raise awareness of the homeless, the addicted, the broken and those in need. Through simple acts of kindness, we can make a difference."*
>
> **— Lance Pearce**

A Near Fatal Decision

By Michael Edgar

My journey included doing young and dumb things. I grew up in a way that I thought was normal. At one point in my life, almost 10 years ago, I was extremely depressed. I had an excessive amount of self-hatred. When you combine self-loathing with alcohol and drugs, it is a recipe for disaster- like throwing fuel on a fire.

I had become disabled and suffered from a spinal injury, so I had very limited use of my legs. In an effort to manage my pain, I began taking pain medications. The physical pain made my existing emotional and mental pain relentless and unbearable. Self-medicating was the only escape I had.

I didn't want to be in a wheelchair and walking with a cane. I felt useless, helpless, and incapable. I didn't want to be pitied, resented, or have others see me as "different". When people looked at me, they stood face to face with just one of the many fears that they held deep within themselves. I was a walking "what if" that made people stop in their tracks with discomfort. To others, I was just another casualty in society. Of course, there were a select group of people who reached out to me for no other reason than to help, but my self-loathing caused me to interpret their kindness to mean that I was a pitied and helpless victim.

Although I battled with discouragement and frustration, the real problem was that I didn't feel like I had any real worth or value. I honestly felt like my life was no longer worth living.

I was slowly losing control and spiraling into a pit of hopelessness and despair. One day, I decided I was DONE. I found my way to a spot and took a bunch of oxycotin and pain medicine so that it would take my life. I was done living this life of misery. In a haze, I found myself laying on a bench. I just kept taking more and more pills waiting for my consciousness to fade.

Before I could slip away into oblivion, I was discovered by my wife and brother-in-law who had become concerned that they had not heard from me and decided to go out looking for me. Somehow an internal alarm had been sounded within each of them- separately- and they both felt an urgent push to search for me. They bumped into each other at the park. I was on a bench behind a building and there was no way for anyone to see me. Yet, they both found me at the same time on this obscure bench. They immediately called an ambulance and it saved my life.

I ended up in the hospital for a period of time.

I had hit rock bottom.

I knew that I had to get away from certain people because, at that point in my life, nothing good could come from our association. More importantly, I had to work on myself. I went away to heal for a few weeks. During that period, I separated myself from the medication, the drugs, and the lifestyle. It was like ripping an entire person out of me.

I came face to face with all my habits, errors in thinking and coping mechanisms. I was left alone to do nothing but think and suffer- physically, mentally, and emotionally. It was painful in a spiritual way. It was like the old me was being ripped out of my body in order to make room for the new me.

During this time, I faced the worst battle I had ever gone through. All my pain was front and center, and I had no substances to numb me from feeling everything. It was even worse than the mental anguish that led me to attempt suicide. It was just something inside tearing at me. I sat in my pain and it was excruciating, and then I was released from it.

Surviving this process eventually led me to a drug and alcohol free existence. The thing about substance abuse is that it becomes a lifestyle and it isn't always easy to completely unplug from the social settings where the substance abuse took place. Yes, I avoid those old settings but, ironically, I'm more social now that I ever was. I am free to be vulnerable and transparent in my relationships because I am no longer consumed with masking my pain. Now, I associate that old lifestyle with pain. I don't choose pain.

I used to feel hopeless. The thing about hopelessness is that it discounts the reality that every situation is subject to change and there is ALWAYS something to be thankful for. Hopelessness is a LIE. There are NO hopeless situations. No matter how many hard days, months or years have passed, we can always hope as long as there is a new day.

Before my suicide attempt, my pride kept me from expressing what was truly on my mind and in my heart. I numbed my pain, hurts and disappointments and it almost cost me my life. Had I succeeding in killing myself, I would have missed out on the last 10 years of my life that have been incredible. I thank God every day that I survived.

I am now a Pastor that finds joy in sharing my story with others to encourage them and point them to the cross. To see the lives that have been changed through the testimony I have told has been a highlight of my life. I am also the owner of a coffee place and I get to bring joy and comfort to people every day. I almost robbed myself, my family and so many other people of that with one really bad choice. Those depressed feelings were temporary, but suicide is permanent.

Had I succeeded in killing myself, I would have never had an opportunity to witness my wife's willingness to stand by my side in the darkest of times. I would have never lived to bring my four amazing sons into this world. I love my sons so much and can't imagine a world without them. Moreover, my anguish prevented me from seeing how devastating my death would have been on those around me. I have been blessed so much.

I've been sober for so long that I sometimes forget that there was a time when I was completely controlled by substances. I strongly believe that God supernaturally broke the stronghold of substance abuse over my life. He transformed and restored me. Through it all, I have maintained my sobriety. And it has not always been easy. At first, I had a hard time identifying as anything other than an alcoholic but alcoholism or being a drug addict should never be an identifier.

Alcoholism does NOT define me. My past does NOT define me.

The bible says it is no longer I who lives, but Christ who lives in me. The life that I now live is because the son of God gave his life for me. What defines me is Christ and Christ alone. Not who I once was, but who I was created to be. After all that I have been through, I know that I can overcome anything through Christ who strengthens me.

I went from being in a wheelchair to experiencing a full recovery physically, emotionally, mentally, and spiritually. Had I not been open to speaking what was on my heart when I finally sought help, I would not be here. Don't ever be afraid or ashamed to talk to other people about what is going on inside of you. It takes courage to ask for help. There is always somebody you can talk to, who cares and will help if you ask for help.

Transformation Tip

You have so much more to offer than what you think drugs or alcohol are offering. You are more than enough without all of those things. Think about someone who is next to you who might also be struggling and how much you can influence them when they see you living a better life without having to touch any of that. Remember, that most people next to you are also hurting. If not, then they are about to go through something. When you are sober and strong, you can help more people.

Michael Edgar *is the owner of Yellow Mug, a coffee shop in Fresno, California. His wife, Crystal, and his boys are the greatest joy in his life. He is a pastor and can be reached at <u>yellowmugrlc@gmail.com</u> or www.yellowmug.coffee*

4

Family Matters

One Decision that Changed My Family Forever

By Clara Hinton

It was midnight and I was just about closing down my computer when the email came through. The subject line read, "Description of a Pedophile." Odd. Very odd, especially since I wasn't really sure of what a pedophile was, not to mention the fact that this email came from the room down the hallway.

I read the description of a pedophile not knowing what was about to happen. Slowly, I walked to my youngest daughter's room, opened the door, and there she was looking like a tiny ball of brokenness clutching her knees, tears falling down her face. "What's going on? What does this email mean? What do you want to tell me?" I asked as I held her shaking body against me.

"Mom, I can't hold it in anymore. I watched dad taking those little girls to the park to go swimming and I can't live with myself if I don't tell. Dad is a pedophile."

My head began spinning a million miles a second. "Dad is a pedophile." "I need to tell." "I can't hold it in anymore." For a brief moment I believe I experienced what insanity feels like. I'd been a preacher's wife for almost forty years. We had a family that was often referred to as the model family. Eleven children -- every one of them active members of the church, college educated, bright, intelligent, well-adjusted kids. Every single one. No! This couldn't be possible. This can't be happening. Not our family. Not us. No! No! No!

This happened around the time that news of Jerry Sandusky hit the newspapers. That was a huge headline quite unlike today when we see news of sexual abuse daily. We are much more educated now. Abuse is being reported more frequently. And, we have far more resources available now than ever before. I was already envisioning how immense this news would be if this were true. In that moment of seeming partial insanity my thoughts were reeling.

Holding my daughter tightly against me to the point of feeling her heart beating against mine, I made a decision that I knew would change her life, my life, and the lives of every one of her siblings forever. I knew this decision would be far-reaching into the community changing the lives of all of the church members who adored the man I married. I knew that this decision would forever bring pain into the lives of those I loved.

And, then I spoke three life-altering words in a voice that was clear and concise. "I believe you."

Alex melted into my arms and we sobbed into the wee hours of the morning. Alex shared with me that her dad had abused her when she was young. She never told as is the case in the majority of abuse cases. Shame. Guilt. Fear. Feelings of unworthiness. And, the most overriding fear of all is that of not being believed.

The events that followed next were nothing short of a series of one painful step after another. The first step was to go to Jimmy, my son that took over his dad's place in the pulpit. Jimmy was now preaching in the very same church where his dad had ministered Sunday after Sunday for close to forty years. How does a mother explain the screams of a broken heart coming from her child? Jimmy modeled his life after his father's. To hear these words about the man he most respected aside from God cut through Jimmy's heart like a knife draining out every last ounce of life from his heart.

Jimmy and I met privately and knew what the next step would be. We went to see our local police. Terrified, not knowing what to expect, we told of the events of the past twenty-four hours. We cried. We buried our heads in shame feeling as though we had let down Alex and any others who had been harmed by this man. Already we were beginning to distance our emotions from him. We knew this was the only way we could rationally make it through the harrowing days, weeks, and months to follow. The officer took the information and after talking with Alex, Jimmy, and myself separately had enough to begin a formal investigation.

Next came the hardest part yet. We had to tell the rest of the family -- no easy task when the family is large and lives in several different states. So, Jimmy and I split the family down the center. He would call each one on his list, and I'd call those on mine. There were screams of horror and disbelief. Some ran to the bathroom to throw up. One of my sons had a violent reaction to the news and said he was driving to town to find his dad to kill him.

Days on end of no sleep, very little eating, stress off the charts, and not being able to share with others took its toll in the form of nightmares for most of us. How would we maneuver this? Thankfully, the investigation only took six weeks. There was enough hard-core evidence to arrest John and put him behind bars on a bail bond of $300,000. He didn't deny anything, neither did he think that he had done anything too wrong. He willingly went to jail thinking in his mind that he would be out in a day or two.

News of John's arrest was huge, hitting newspapers as far as three states away. There were over 200 counts including rape, possession of child pornography, and molestation of victims as young as four-years-old. **For reference: https://www.tribdem.com/news/local_news/2-charged-in-separate-sex-cases-involving-minors/article_65f35238-ff19-5f9e-9581-d2e87c88fca2.html

Our family was no longer the model family. We were broken beyond belief. In the split second it took to say "I believe you" our lives changed dramatically and will never be the same. But, something else happened during that *defining moment*. I learned the true value of doing the right thing no matter the cost. In the end, when we do what is right, there are immeasurable blessings that follow.

This has been a ten year journey of healing for us. John is in prison where he will remain for life with no chance of parole. We learned that he did molest other daughters in the family, each one believing she was the only one. Alex, the youngest child, taught all of us the value of one voice. Because of her courage to speak out and risking not being believed, countless other children have been saved from the lifetime pain of abuse.

We've grown closer as a family during this time of brokenness. We learned just how strong our love for each other is, and we've formed a bond of support that is amazing. There are still areas of brokenness that need to be healed and we are working on those.

As a woman, wife, and mother, I learned that I have an inner strength that is fueled by love and sustained by God. I had no idea how I would take on the role of both mother and father, of being the sole proprietor of our finances, and of guiding the spiritual nurturing of children and grandchildren, and yet it's happening. A faith-based foundation will not crumble even under the pressure of the harshest storms. I was a timid country woman who learned how to speak up for myself and my family. I'm so proud to say that I even set up an appointment with the president of our bank and asked for some leniency for three months until I collected my thoughts and figured out finances. I learned that people at the top are wonderful and will work with you when you are truthful!

This has not been an easy journey by any means, nor is it over. There is still grief over the loss of the father that the children loved. Since this happened, our family experienced the sudden death of my oldest son, Mike. He died of a heart attack leaving behind his wife and three young children. Many lonely nights were spent in bed crying alone, having nobody to share the grief. Every holiday, every birthday, every special event is a reminder that we are not whole. Yet, we are also reminded that we are healing, and that's what gives us the hope needed to continue on.

About five years after the initial shock of that email, I decided to begin writing about my journey as the wife of a pedophile. That opened many doors of support for me. Shortly after I began writing, my son Jimmy began writing about his experiences as a son of a pedophile. Those two ways of reaching out gave Jimmy and I the realization that there are thousands suffering through the mental, physical, and spiritual fatigue and trauma of abuse. After putting our heads together, we decided to do a weekly podcast called "Speaking Out on Sexual Abuse." Needless to say, this podcast has increased our opportunities of offering others help who are just beginning this journey that we began over ten years ago.

We might think our one voice doesn't count. Just think of what one young girl's voice did! Because Alex spoke out, thousands of others now are protected and receive support. You might think that the truth is too hard. It's not. Those three words, "I believe you" proved to me that the truth is always the right decision. I have grown into a woman of strength, and I am so happy to say that. You might think that broken families can never heal. I'm here to tell you that from the ashes can come untold beauty. Our family was not just broken. We were shredded, and we are finding healing in so many beautiful ways, and so will you! You will never be left so weak you cannot stand when you build your foundation and trust in heavenly ways. The truth always wins. Many times, our greatest strengths come from our weakest moments!

Transformation Tip

If you are in an abusive situation, seek someone who will believe you. Use your voice. You are worthy. You have far more strength than you can imagine. Take that first step towards your physical, spiritual, or mental freedom. Help is available. There are food banks, women's shelters, helplines, podcasts, blogs, and many groups that meet to provide help and guidance. I didn't know where to begin to look. Start with your inner circle of closest friends. Then, seek out local services in your community. And, look online for information and support. You don't need to be a victim of abuse. Instead, become a thriving survivor of abuse. You can do it!

Clara Hinton is best known for her work in grief associated with child loss as well as her advocacy work with sexual abuse. She is the author of Hope 365: Daily Meditations for the Grieving Heart https://amzn.to/3fjvRq1

She also has a podcast with her son, Jimmy, called: Speaking Out on Sexual Abuse https://www.spreaker.com/show/the-speaking-out-on-abuse-show *or* https://jimmyhinton.org/podcast/

Learn more about Clara at: https://www.silentgriefsupport.com/ *and* https://findingahealingplace.com/

Surviving to Thriving

By Alicia Anne

Trudging through life's valleys is a beautiful mess of a process. It's a process I walked through personally and wondered, often, whether I would come out on the other side with my own sanity. By God's grace, I did.

The condensed version of the first part of my journey began with a marriage that was destined to fail, two diagnosed autoimmune diseases, and eight pregnancy losses. I was lucky enough to have my rainbow baby, who is now seven years old. But I still had hope for a second child, even as the foundation of my very world was slowly crumbling beneath me. I thought the worst was behind me, but I was wrong.

A Transition of Faith

The second wave hit me harder than the first. For more than 30 years of my life, I stood my ground defending the things I was sure of. Even as the promise of children slipped through my fingers, painful loss after painful loss, I remained faithful to a warped theology that I would eventually abandon for a faith so much deeper than I ever believed possible.

My body was broken. My faith was broken. I began seeing evidence of things which I didn't want to believe. They couldn't possibly be what they appeared to be, but I was in denial. Eventually I had to accept that my marriage, too, was broken, and well beyond repair. My efforts to repair it were in vain.

And Then There Was More

In the middle of trying to fix what I mistakenly believed were my own deficiencies in my marriage, I unexpectedly became pregnant with my tenth pregnancy. Things at home grew worse and instead of the joy I should have felt, all I could feel was dread. I took pregnancy test after pregnancy test, hoping that the line would begin to fade as it had for so many other pregnancies before.

I fought a battle in my mind against terminating my pregnancy. I was staunchly pro-life, which is an easy position to support when you've never been in a desperate situation. This time, however, I found myself trying to bypass my conscience to somehow justify what I felt I needed to do. I felt panicked, helpless, and hopeless.

There was no way I could bring a baby into this mess. How could I support myself and two young children? There's no way a loving God would ask me to do this. And yet, test after test, the line continued to grow darker. I was confirmed to be with child and the due date was January 12 – the same date I found out my firstborn had died inside my womb. How cruel was this God?

My thoughts eventually turned to believing that maybe God would use this baby to restore my broken marriage. I was an optimist, so in that spirit, I planned a wonderful Father's Day afternoon trip to the coast to share the news with my four-year-old and then-husband. I was blindsided by the response I got.

It wasn't the first time the marriage covenant was cheapened with controlling threats. It was demanded that I give up all rights to name the baby, with no possible discussion or compromise over the name, and told that if I didn't oblige, the marriage would be over.

He declared (without any medical evidence) that it was a boy, and that it was the man's "Biblical right" as the head of the household to name the children. Due to personal convictions, I disagreed with the name he wanted. I was devasted. I drove the three of us home from that trip; a broken heart, a restless child in the back, and an angry and drunk passenger who eventually fell asleep. I prayed, "Please God, let this be a girl."

It's a Boy

I wasn't given a girl. In fact, in a quiet moment, the name "Josiah" came clearly to mind. I tucked it away, still unwilling to believe that God would put me through a battle over the name of a boy. It was later confirmed that I was carrying a healthy boy, and I clearly knew what his name would be: Josiah, which translates to: Jehovah Heals.

My marriage did not heal. Things became worse. The month after Father's Day, I got photographic evidence of what I already knew in my heart was happening. I also got a cold confession. Even so, I held onto fragile hope that the confession was a sign of things turning around, but it wasn't.

Seeking Help

From the advice of friends, I sought help to get out of my situation. It would be almost four months living with the secret that I was leaving before help with housing was available.

When I finally left, the nightmare exploded. A community of people I'd spent the past 13 years calling "family", seemed to turn on me without warning. My reputation was tarnished by whatever insidious stories had circulated in the void I left when I shut down my social media. I witnessed some of the most hurtful things said about me, yet I chose to remain silent. This was by far, more painful than the disintegration of my marriage.

A paternity test had also been requested, and at once I began to understand a little of the peculiar behavior of some of my previously closest friends. It was in that moment that I made the pivotal decision that my integrity would have to stand on its own or not at all. I would not fight to keep people in my life who would accept the possibility that such stories were true without any thread of merit behind their belief.

I had already mourned the loss of my health, eight of my children and my father; now I would mourn the loss of my hopes for a fitness career, my husband, my home, my community, and my faith. I was at a deficit, living in a home not my own with a soon-to-be newborn and a four-year-old, making $300 a month of self-employment income, and torn between the choice of bonding with my newborn or getting out there to look for a job to support them.

The Upward Turn

Today, I've found a healthier, egalitarian faith and a new church community at VIA Church in my community. With help from social services, community resources, a supportive church and loving friends and family, I completed my Paralegal Associates degree and Certificate in Fall of 2020 with Dean's List recognition. I was also recently hired to work for a small-but-mighty law firm; an amazing miracle in the midst of a pandemic.

I plan to use my learned skills to both advocate for victims of domestic violence and to provide a comfortable and stable life for my children.

The Most Incredible Miracle – My Mom, My Hero

My mother was my advocate through everything and desperately wanted for her daughter and grandsons to have stability and a home. I suffered one more loss when she suddenly passed away. The last conversation my kids and I had with my mother was Easter 2019 over video chat. Just a few short hours after our conversation, she suffered severe medical complications rendering her minimally responsive and on life support. Though incredibly painful and I miss her dearly, she - along with help from my grandparents - provided for the most incredible miracle that I never saw coming. With the small inheritance she left, we moved back into the family home where the boys and I now have an affordable place to live for this season and on into the next.

Transformation Tip

One of the most profound pieces of advice that got me through with my sanity intact was given to me by my therapist: "You cannot change others, nor should you try. You can only change yourself." This simple truth invited me to consider my real options instead of waiting on the "what ifs," and empowered me to develop healthier boundaries. My therapist also taught me the critical skill of separating my emotions from my decisions by stepping back and approaching every choice as a business transaction. I still grieved deeply, but this skill ultimately helped me make the best decisions for my boys and me.

When it came to my faith, I had to be willing to deconstruct three decades of theology and risk losing it all to finally find a raw and real deity who cared deeply for women just as much as he did for men. What doubts might you have? Go ahead and challenge your faith – God can handle it.

> *"Truly, I found a bigger God in the valley than I ever would have on the mountain."*
>
> — Alicia Anne

Alicia Anne is a mother of two boys, now seven and two. She and her fiancé Michael are outspoken Christian feminists, offering hope and support to other women and men who are working through similar circumstances. Alicia hopes that her continuing education will strengthen her ability to advocate in her community. She can be reached at aliciaanne1984@gmail.com

---

The Trauma After the Trauma

By Ann Justi

You never know when a moment will turn into a moment that you never forget. You hope that it's a happy moment like a birthday, a wedding, an anniversary, a graduation... but my *defining moment* wasn't happy at all.

I had a good life, in general, even with some horrible experiences in my youth. I had been in some terrible car accidents. In the 1970's, through grade school and high school, I was bullied and even beaten by the other students. At age 17, I lost my virginity to a date rape. Two years later, I was robbed and shot at. In four more years, I nearly died from a serious illness. All of that was before I met my husband.

I was settling into our new home after being married just four months. I was making business calls and getting our budget in order. I made the mistake of using my maiden name and not my newly married name on a call. My husband overheard it. Oops.

He started with yelling at me, then progressed to hitting and kicking. Except for victims of sex trafficking, most victims of domestic violence indicate that the abuse escalated over time. Some describe it starting with a reactive or "accidental" slap. Perhaps a shove or a push that was just a little too rough. An object thrown or a door slammed while they were standing in the doorway. Never zero to 100.

That is definitely not my story.

My first experience being physically abused left me with a broken nose, a broken palate, bruising throughout my lower body and (though I didn't know it right away) permanent damage to one of my inner ears, causing hearing loss that would never return. I honestly thought he was going to kill me.

I consider myself lucky in that, at the time, I was resourceful, employed, had a network of friends and knew that my injuries were so grave, that this was unacceptable. I was able to get free and put an emergency action plan in place quickly; it helped that I have a career background in disaster recovery.

My husband's assault on me wasn't my defining moment. No, that didn't come until later, after I was safe, with an order of protection in place, and he was incarcerated; it shocked me to my core. Normally, I am a high-functioning person, the kind who works through injuries, illness or tiredness, despite many obstacles that may be in the way. I was the person you count on when all hell breaks loose.

My injuries had been treated and my husband was awaiting sentencing. I woke up and had to go to work, the same as I had been doing for six days a week, often working double shifts. But something wasn't right; I didn't feel right, deep inside. I did not want to leave the house. I thought that something was wrong. I was on high alert, akin to when you hear someone about to break into your home late at night. I felt that any random stranger I encountered might hurt me. I didn't want anyone touching me.

This was not me. I was the person who could get through anything. I had dealt with injuries before - a broken nose from a car accident, other bangs, and bruises from childhood. But this time, something was different; something not physical or visible but very real.

I managed to go to work, bringing liquids for lunch. I couldn't chew or drink through a straw. It even hurt to drink from a cup. Normally extremely outgoing, I stopped talking to people unless absolutely necessary. I didn't know what was going on but thought I would get over it. This was 2004; post-traumatic stress disorder (PTSD) was still relatively unheard of, not yet the stuff of headlines and war stories. PTSD is an anxiety disorder that involves the over-activation of the fight and flight response.

When it didn't pass, after a week, I called my insurer and asked to see a mental health provider. I described my symptoms (the trauma triggers developed later). Their response was that I had to tell them what mental illness I had, or they couldn't help me. But I couldn't - I didn't know and neither did anyone else who was helping me.

I didn't want to go back to my physician because it was a busy time at work so taking off more than the few days I took after the assault would've been a burden on the staff. I tried to research my symptoms. I didn't know of any domestic violence victims help groups or shelters. I didn't know what to say to the insurer, or of any private therapists that could diagnose me. I didn't want people to think I was crazy, but something was definitely not right.

I finally called my insurer back and said it must be panic attacks; they booked me an evaluation. The evaluating therapist determined that I had PTSD but did not explain it to me and thought that having time away from my husband and talking about the incident would help me. It did the opposite. I didn't want to relive that again; I missed the husband I fell in love with, not the man who had attacked me. So, I had to figure it out myself.

Since my husband drank, a friend suggested that I try Al-Anon; a support group for the relatives of people suffering from alcoholism. I'd stopped taking regular yoga and meditation classes when my husband wanted me to attend to his needs, so I decided to take them again. I was willing to try anything to calm myself. The therapist had suggested group counseling with other domestic violence victims, but it didn't help me because my story was not like theirs and no one mentioned having problems with PTSD. (I think many of them didn't know the signs or were still in survival mode.)

I was having success with Al-Anon, despite being a silent observer in the meetings (very atypical of me before the assault). They gave me peace, as I listened to how others were changing themselves and the way they looked at living with an alcoholic. The yoga and meditation helped as well; I just had to follow the directions and not do anything for anyone but me. It gave me time to listen to God and my body.

Someone at my local Westchester yoga class suggested that I try Kundalini yoga classes at a specific studio in Manhattan. I started going most weekdays and going to my local classes on the weekend. The Kundalini studio advertised a yoga Rebirthing class, designed specifically for overcoming unresolved problems with pain and fear. I tried it, following it up with classes in Sacred Therapies, Kundalini yoga mediations for mental health and more. Rebirthing classes were for removing the baggage of the past, all collectively known as yoga therapy. I got dramatically better, learning how to move forward in my life and continue working without reliving the trauma, without my husband and without a complete distrust of strangers.

Kundalini yoga therapy works on the subconscious. To quote the founding teacher, Yogi Bhajan, "The idea of Rebirthing is to release the subconscious, the storehouse of misery." Another of his quotes that resonates for me is, "If your subconscious is totally cleared and clean, you'll be doing totally different things, and you will be a lot happier and more effective than you are today."

My healing and understanding approached a culmination when one of my yoga teachers suggested that I become a teacher myself, since I had studied yoga at an ashram for five years when I was younger - long before meeting my husband. I studied and earned my yoga teaching certificate but, without experience, I was having trouble finding a side job teaching yoga. The only people who reached out to me were people who had trouble attending regular classes due to issues they had with mental health or physical limitations. I studied specifically how to help those types of clients and took yoga therapy teaching classes.

This was a *defining moment* for me - I used my resourcefulness and worked to help myself overcome my PTSD when traditional methods didn't work, then I used those skills I learned to become a teacher and help others with PTSD and other mental and physical issues.

Once I felt ready to look for romantic partners again, I chose to be upfront about my past trauma, without any shame or embarrassment - I was a survivor. My story has a great ending; I am now happily married to a fellow domestic violence survivor who is male (yes, it does happen), whom I'm very grateful to for accepting me as I am and giving me a safe home. I am grateful for many people in my life. For instance, I thank the friend who sheltered me, saving my life, and another who helped me relocate. I've learned that my life is more important than any possession or relationship.

Transformation Tip

The symptoms of PTSD vary from person to person, depending on how long ago the trauma occurred, the type of trauma, your history of trauma and resilience. However, general symptoms from PTSD include the following: a significant change in physical and emotional reactions, nightmares and sleep problems, avoidance of interacting or things associated with the trauma, feeling "on guard" most of the time and invasive upsetting memories or flashbacks of the trauma.

Not everyone who experiences trauma develops PTSD. If you feel something is not normal for you- GET HELP.

For immediate help, text the Crisis Text Line-

Text: HOME to 741741 to connect with a crisis counselor.

Find a trauma informed counselor at:

www.psychologytoday.com/us/therapists/trauma-and-ptsd

Join an in-person or online peer PTSD support group. You are not alone, and support helps the healing process.

Add to your recovery with complementary and alternative therapies. I found doing several things to help my PTSD relieved it quicker and more completely in the long term.

Ann Justi *has been a yoga therapist for over 10 years specializing in mental health including PTSD and physical limitation issues. She is a certified master desire life coach who assists clients on an individual and group basis in designing relationships, lifestyle desires and finding their true identity. She also speaks at events and produces mastermind groups as well as educational seminars. If you suspect that you or someone you know is suffering from PTSD and would like more information, contact Ann at* DevotedYoga@gmail.com *or go online to* YourDesiredLifeCoaching.com *or DevotedYoga.net*

An Oscar Worthy Performance

By Shannon P. Murree

My story began over twenty years ago when I landed my "dream job" in another country. It didn't have snow like my city in Canada but who wouldn't want to live in sunny and warm Mexico? As a woman in my 20s, I was enjoying my independence and the unique experiences my life offered. Along the way, I fell in love with and married a co-worker. Unfortunately, the honeymoon didn't last long.

In our first few months of wedded bliss, life seemed fantastic, but little did I realize things were changing. Sometimes, he would express little insecurities and control. During that first year, my father came to visit. I recall we were trying to decide where to go for dinner and my husband stormed off, leaving my dad and me alone. I shrugged my shoulders thinking nothing of it, but this raised alarm bells to my dad. He expressed his concern about some controlling actions & comments he witnessed. I just got defensive and made excuses saying that he was probably just tired after a long day of work.

Then one day I happily announced we were pregnant. The first sign…control. Simple tasks like going to the local store to get milk or bread caused so much conflict and unnecessary fights. Sometimes that led to things being aggressively yanked from my hands, a small shove or doors being slammed. I was a dance choreographer and suddenly the costumes required were "too revealing". For the sake of delivering a healthy baby, "we" decided it was time for me to stop performing on stage since he believed it to be "too risky". Instead, I would become a stay-at-home mom and he'd care for us.

When I share my story, people are shocked by the fact that I never saw the signs. Perhaps I was in denial. However, looking back, it seems that announcing my pregnancy was the incident that prompted this sudden, but significant, change. Somehow, after I became pregnant, I was no longer me. I was instantly deemed a mom, the woman carrying his child and like some delicate token in a china shop. I was to be protected, admired but not touched (ironic). I was his pride (NOT prized) possession.

It was odd how normal activities caused instant rage and accusations. I was constantly put in the position of defending myself and trying to diffuse his rage if I took too long at the local store. This made going out unbearable. The accusations of cheating or doing things out of my character were escalating beyond my comprehension so I would tiptoe around and eventually stopped doing things that I knew would upset him. It was extremely challenging as I was a caring, reasonable, respectful, and independent woman. Despite this, I noticed my demeanor start to change just to keep the peace.

The first time...I never saw it coming.

I recall that I took too long at the store again. I had innocently talked to the store owner as she asked how I was feeling. I rushed home (only a few houses away) apologetic and fearful to cause another fight. This time I barely got the groceries out of my hand when "WHACK", right across my face without warning. The shock, the anger, the humiliation that ensued is indescribable. Never had I ever- in all my life- experienced physical abuse and, in my mind, I refused to start now!

I remember lashing back with my words and screaming, "*Who the heck do you think you are??!!*" In hindsight, confronting a physically abusive person like that was not the best thing to do as it prompted another assault across my face. I retreated to the second bedroom sobbing uncontrollably and afraid. He came in, apologized, and fed me every excuse in the book. "Something happened at work...your disrespect was the last straw...besides, you're supposed to know not to take so long at the store." Since it had never happened before, we kissed, we hugged, and I forgave him. We moved on.

Months passed before a second undeniable incident of abuse happened. At the time of the second incident, our first son had already been born and I was pregnant with our second child. The tension in our city was intense because we were under a State of Emergency and tornado watch. Keep in mind our house was on slab, no basement, only a small, two bedroom home and nowhere to go, making tensions in our home even more unbearable. I was in the hallway trying to calm our crying child as we were all scared. I also didn't want to disturb "the dragon". I secretly deemed him such because I never knew when he'd unleash his fire.

Unfortunately, my efforts did not work and, as I muttered something along the lines of, "I'm trying to hush our child", the dragon was not satisfied with this response. I refrained from arguing but perhaps the look in my eyes said it all. All I remember is the demonic look and his response at punching himself in the face all the while yelling and saying that this is what I would probably like to do. It was like he became possessed.

As I backed up in shock, I stumbled, and he proceeded to shift the assaults onto me while I held our child. I took the hits to protect our son. I remember crying myself to sleep that night in my son's room with a knife under my pillow as protection. We made up the next morning of course because it was the "stress" of the situation. This time he agreed to go to counselling.

The last incident that I recall occurred when we were visiting his parents in another state. Whatever set him off (it didn't take much) and whatever confidence I had with witnesses around caused me to shout back. When that familiar sting went across my face, I looked at his mom for words of protection. Instead, I was chastised for talking back to her son and not "knowing my place." In fact, I was blatantly told to "never talk back to your husband." *That was it. I was done.* At that moment-*my defining moment*- I decided I would not allow my one-year-old son and unborn daughter to think this type of behavior was acceptable.

After seeing that this behavior was deemed as warranted by the matriarch of the family, I refused to let this pattern continue to the next generation. Many conversations happened from this incident and, when I told him I was leaving him, he told me definitively that I could leave but not with our son. *I was devastated but what could I do?* At that moment, I would do anything to ensure the safety of our child. So, I lied and told him that we'd be a family forever.

Not my proudest moment, but certainly the best acting of my life. By lying, I had violated my moral code. But by honoring my promise and staying in this abusive and disrespectful relationship, I would be violating myself. *I knew what I had to do.*

Eventually, I was able to convince him that obvious stresses were causing the demise of our relationship and, if he would permit me (right- "permit") to make some changes, I would create a wonderful, new life for us. I convinced him that my home country of Canada would have better opportunities for us and provide a fresh start.

Shockingly, he agreed to move. I pretended to look for jobs for both of us. I should have won an academy award! After months of planning "our" new life and as I was approaching my third trimester of pregnancy, I told him that there were just a few loose ends that needed to be tied up in Canada. My husband did contract work and could not leave Mexico until his contracts were up. Knowing this, I told him, "They won't let me fly in my third trimester, so we (my son and I) will just fly out there and get things ready for you." He agreed and signed paperwork allowing me to take our son out of the country.

Check Mate.

From time to time, I re-live the moment I left him. I recall vividly having my one-year-old child in my arms, pregnant with our daughter and nothing but the clothes on our backs and one suitcase. As the plane took off, a feeling of relief and liberation swept over me!

I had arranged to live with my grandparents. They lived in a bungalow and could offer me a small room in the basement. That was all we needed: freedom and a place, safe from the nightmare we had lived, to lay down our heads at night. I had such a strong sense of independence that it felt irrelevant that I opted to bathe my son in a laundry basket in our section of the home instead of doing it in the shared bathroom upstairs.

Growing up, my grandfather would always say, "If you don't look out for you and take care of you first, how can you expect anyone else to? You have to put yourself as number 1." I was grateful to have a support system, and I knew he was right. Ultimately, it was my responsibility to create a good life for me and my children. I knew I needed to "find myself" again and implement self-care. For a long time, I didn't confide in anyone because I was so embarrassed and ashamed that I, a strong, independent woman, would allow this to happen. I had compromised everything I knew and believed in for the sake of having a relationship. It was not love, or at least, not my version of it.

When I was with my husband, we lived a comfortable life financially. Now, I was starting from nothing. It was hard but I didn't care. No amount of money was worth compromising our safety. Step by step, I managed to get back on my feet. It was a process, but I was able to rebuild.

For months before I left, I had to live a lie, play the game, and do everything necessary to focus on the win: my escape. It was revolting, but to cross country lines with my son legally, it was what I had to do. I managed to survive and escape. Years later, I successfully raised that boy and girl to become well-meaning and established young adults and individuals.

Today, I run a successful real estate business with an amazing team that generates millions of dollars in sales each year. I have been able to use the tenacity and strength that allowed me to escape and build a successful business to evolve.

I feel very empowered and am extremely involved in many philanthropic endeavors. I have turned my personal story into a "why" and find strength and purpose in sharing it. I support various women's initiatives that focus on 1.) supporting the financial literacy and independence of women, 2.) creating awareness about gender-based violence and child abuse and 3.) sharing stories to empower and encourage others.

We can take adversity and allow it to fuel us while healing and helping others. When we do this, we ultimately become even more empowered. I have found peace in equipping women with the resources they need to regain control to live a safe and happy life.

Transformation Tip

Abuse takes many forms (physical, mental, emotional, sexual, financial etc.) but the underlying theme is always the same- control and manipulation. I didn't recognize it as abuse when my ex-husband turned his violence on himself - but it was. It was an attempt to perplex and frighten me so he could control my behavior. Abuse can be complicated and even subtle at times. When someone threatens to harm themselves if you terminate your relationship with them, they are holding you hostage emotionally - that's abuse. The best way to protect yourself from abuse of any form is to know and recognize the signs so you don't get caught in a cycle of abuse. Even if you feel like something is wrong, despite what the other person is telling you, trust your instinct and don't ignore the signs.

Create a set of personal boundaries concerning the treatment from others that you absolutely will NOT tolerate. These boundaries should protect your mental, physical, emotional, spiritual, and financial health. They should also promote your personal growth and safeguard you from treatment that undermines your inherent dignity and worth as a human being.

For instance, a reasonable personal boundary that serves to protect your emotional well-being might be, "I will not engage with someone who mocks or laughs at me when I express how I feel because my feelings are valid even if that person doesn't think they are justified." If someone crosses this boundary, you could say, "I have a right to feel the way I feel. My feelings are valid - even if you don't agree with them. I'm going to remove myself from this conversation if you don't stop mocking my feelings and I will resume this conversation only when you can approach me as a person with feelings that matter." At that point, the other person is free to choose, and you act accordingly.

In instances when a person blatantly and routinely crosses your personal boundary, depending on the nature of the boundary, you may have to distance yourself from that person or terminate the relationship. When emotions get involved, boundaries serve to help you set a standard for every relationship in your life. It's not easy and you may second guess yourself, but trust the process. Trust the perimeters and standards you've set for yourself because you matter. In any partnership or relationship, though the pendulum may swing from time to time, the bar set for being respected and your integrity should always remain intact. If not, it is time to reconsider that relationship. It is so important, especially early on, to set and honor the standard of what we expect a relationship to be.

Shannon Murree *is a mother, investor, consultant, multi-faceted businesswoman and valued confidante. She is an award winning and licensed REALTOR® with RE/MAX Hallmark Chay Realty Brokerage who speaks province-wide on the benefits of real estate investing, entrepreneurship, women's empowerment, and financial strategies. Consequently, she is considered a great connector and resource. Shannon finds joy in helping people empower themselves with various wealth creation strategies and strives to make a difference through her real estate business, notable charity work, activism, and philanthropy. She can be reached by email at shannonmurree@gmail.com*

I Never Knew You Were in There

By Alicia Dias

I was adopted as an infant back in 1969. My mother and father made every sacrifice for my brother and me to ensure that our lives were full, beautiful, and exciting. I grew up being so grateful that my biological parents chose to give me life when there were clearly other options. I had always hoped that one day I would be able to thank them for the decision that they made and let them know that my life was perfect. Growing up with this appreciation for family and understanding the important role that parents play in the lives of their children, my adult family naturally took on the dynamic that was modeled to me as a child- intact. My husband and I adored our daughter. And my mother? She was my best friend. I was on top of the world.

On January 1, 2013, if you would have told me that- in just one year- I would lose my mother, that my amazing marriage would completely fall apart AND that, in just 14 months, I would become a full-time, single mom living on food stamps, I would have called you crazy!

But that is exactly what happened to me.

In May of 2013, I lost my mother and best friend as she died in my arms. The last words she spoke to me were, "Wait. I'm not ready."

Her words still haunt me.

Within weeks of her death, my marriage suddenly started to twist and turn, and I found myself alone taking care of my daughter because my husband was suddenly rarely home.

By October, I discovered that the man who declared he could "never cheat on someone" had two relationships with other women-- simultaneously. He even took them to our home to have sex while I was at work running our business.

Three months later, in January, 2014, our impending divorce prevented me from being able to go to work at OUR business. So, just like that, I was out of a job. I had no financial support, so I had to apply for food stamps. I respect anyone who has had to apply for this program as it is humbling and I'm thankful for it because I know it helps so many people. But me- a college graduate with a master's degree who had worked as long I could remember? Suddenly, I found myself faced with thousands of dollars in bills for our household and *no income.* At 44 years old, this was a position I never thought I would find myself in. Who knew?

So there I was, living in California just my daughter and me, with no family in town (or anywhere around), no job, a mountain of bills and the only person that I was going to be able to count on was staring at me in disbelief in the mirror. Had it been just me, I could have easily slumped to the floor and laid in a fetal position for days on end. I was completely isolated (my nearest family member lived two states away), with no idea of what I was going to do. However, assuming the fetal position was not an option for me; I had a 4-year-old who counted on me and there was no way in hell I was going to let her down.

The business we had was an insurance agency so, when I couldn't go back to work, I reached out to our district manager and he encouraged me to open my own agency.

Huh?

I had no sales talent whatsoever!

I grew up in the accounting world and had been a CPA (Certified Public Accountant) for almost two decades before having our daughter. We don't do sales! We sit with our heads down behind a desk with our pocket protectors and calculators, right?! I had knowledge of the insurance business because I was able to learn it with my husband while raising our daughter at home and eventually working in the office alongside him once she was in preschool. But I just did the numbers stuff; he was the one out there doing sales; talking to people one on one, face to face.

But my district manager seemed more than confident that I could do it and, with little to no other options, I accepted the challenge. So, on March 17, 2014, I opened my own insurance agency!

I was always one of those women who did very well in business and looked like I had everything going for me. In my more than 20 years as a CPA I was *confident in my knowledge* and loved to teach others. I spoke at huge conferences in front of thousands of people discussing super exciting issues like "Auditing Federal Government Programs"! Yes, I know the title makes you want to puke but you would be surprised to learn how important that is! It's actually a million times easier to talk to a room full of people than talk to someone one on one.

As a child I was *confident in my abilities*. I was an athlete in grade school (soccer, volleyball, and basketball) and I was great. I danced and choreographed in high school and was talented. During my senior year, I learned I could sing and sang at numerous grand occasions. In fact, I still sing to this day.

Despite this, when it came to having *self-confidence*-- confidence in who I was as a person, as a woman, I was in a deficit. I had none. I never had it. Confidence in my knowledge or abilities was tangible in the trophies and accolades I received. But self-confidence is not something you can score or reward. People would often tell me that I was beautiful, and I would thank them but inside I felt like I was *flawed, ugly, substandard...*

That lack of self-confidence coupled with my husband's own insecurities bled through into our relationship so deeply that it was easier for me to literally stare at my shoes most of the time rather than engage people face to face for fear of his accusations that I was cheating or trying to "grab" the attention in the room. I should have listened to my father when he told me that those who accuse are usually the ones who are guilty of doing it themselves.

Yet somehow, I (the same woman who was too timid to stand up for herself in the face of senseless accusations), was now going to run my own business while being a full-time, single mom to my daughter-- the most important person in the world to me. So often, when you are in a situation where failure is not an option, you find out who you really are and what you're really capable of. That is exactly what happened to me: my desire to provide for my daughter caused me to draw from within the strength to persevere.

With my back against the wall, I resolved that one way or another, I would take care of my sweet little girl. I decided I was going to keep us in the house that we were in, that she was going to stay in the activities that she was in, and there was always going to be food on our table, heat in our home and love in our hearts.

About a year after I made this inner vow, while I was picking up my daughter from her preschool, the woman who owned the preschool looked at me and said, "I never knew you were in there. You are so strong and amazing ... so different from how you were years ago when I first met you!" To this day, that is still the greatest compliment I have ever received and believed.

I must admit that what she saw was accurate. I was thriving. By 2017, just three years after opening my insurance agency, I was honored as Agent of the Year in my district (incidentally, my ex-husband was no longer in the business because I took over his agency). In fact, my great performance was so steady that I received the same honor in 2018 and 2019. These were just a few successes in a string of "wins".

In 2018, I wound up purchasing the home that I had been renting for five years. It was extremely fulfilling to know that my hard work had provided a permanent place for my daughter and I to live. I had created the kind of home that, as a child, I hoped my future children would have. And I had done it through my own blood, sweat and tears. And yes, she is still in her same room as she was all those years ago. But the story is not over yet.

My *defining moment* was set in motion in December of 2018, when some of my dear neighbors who had adopted a child told me about the fun they had as a family having their genetics tested.

So, I decided what the heck I'll do it too! I spit in the tube, sent it away and waited for the results to come back. When they came back I was stunned to discover that they not only informed me of ancestral history that was quite different from what I had originally been told but also linked me with two other people in the world as 1st and 2nd cousins. I knew nothing about all of this but found out that this was quite rare.

Curiosity got the best of me, so I reached out to both of my newfound cousins. In just a matter of three days, I was on the phone with the woman who gave birth to me and two of my biological sisters. I learned that, in total, I have an older half-brother and four younger full blood siblings: two brothers and two sisters. And my biological father? He had passed away the year before in 2018. They told me he was never able to forgive himself for giving me up for adoption.

Not only did I speak to them that day but, in April of that year, my daughter and I met my biological mother, my younger brothers and sisters, all their children and a host of their friends. I was finally able to look my biological mother in the eye and thank her for my life. But even more I was able to share with her the fruits of what my life had become:

My success despite the challenges, my beautiful daughter, and the world that I had created for her. And that is when I realized that I had arrived at a place in my life where I felt confident in me. Enduring for my daughter showed me that I was capable and strong. Embracing my past allowed me to love the entirety of my being. All of me-- the work in progress that stares back at me when I look in the mirror each morning. I am "good enough". I had always been. I just never knew that I was in there.

In life, there are moments where you feel that you have come full circle. This was one of those moments for me. We had an incredible week, one almost fifty years in the making. I will never forget our time together.

It turns out that my biological mother had been diagnosed with stage four pancreatic cancer in July of 2017. The fact that she was even still alive in the spring of 2019 was a miracle in and of itself as someone once diagnosed with this usually lives 4-5 months. There are those of us who still believe she was alive waiting to meet me. Soon after meeting us, her health declined dramatically. Eight months after meeting me, she passed away. I know our reunion gave my mother the peace she needed to pass with no questions left unanswered.

Transformation Tip

Life is going to throw a lot at you, but you need to know that YOU control your worth. YOU determine how you are going to react to each situation, and YOU choose whether you will get the best of it or it wins that round. You know if you have found your self-confidence. If someone tells you that you are good looking, or talented or amazing and the little voice inside your head dismisses it and says "Yeah right" or "I wish" then you know it hasn't come to the surface YET. Life will give you chances to find it and I truly mean "find" it because it is inside you. Hopefully, you don't have to go through as much as I did. So, when it's your turn...

- If you ever think you're not good enough, you are.

- If it ever scares you because you're alone it's OK because you're supposed to do it alone.
- Take the time to find the "YOU" that is in there because the world will be a better place seeing the real you and life will be better.

Alicia Dias is the happy mother of an 11-year-old daughter and together they are family with a host of fur babies. She has lived in California since 1998. In addition to being a successful business owner she is an accomplished singer. She can be reached at debitsandcredits@ymail.com

The Road to Nowhere

By Diana Houk

In 1989, I was not happy with my life. I was a single mother with three small children who were totally dependent on me in every area of their lives.

I had been in church and a believer in Jesus Christ my entire life. Nevertheless, life had not always been easy. I had experienced more tragedies, loss, and disappointments than most people do in their lifetime. But, through it all, my faith remained.

One thing my mother taught me was this: when you don't know what to do, you TRUST GOD. So, that's exactly what I did when I found myself at a standstill in my relationship with David. David was a good person and had been raised in church. He had never been married before and didn't have any children but got along with mine.

We had been dating for five years and I had expressed to him after year one that I needed to know that we were on the path towards marriage. He assured me that we would get married "when the time was right". I was satisfied with his vague answer devoid of a specific timeline because, deep down inside, I knew he wasn't the one for me. We were in a very weird place. Our relationship looked good on paper. I was comfortable with him and more than anything I deeply desired that my children eventually grow up in a healthy and balanced family environment- with both a mother and father in the home. Looking back, I think I carried with me a subconscious insecurity that being a single mother was an undesirable trait to potential suitors. *I had found a nice man who cared for me and my children...shouldn't that be enough?*

But David and I had our differences--differences that seemed miniscule and easy enough to overlook but served as subtle reminders that the relationship wasn't what I *really* wanted. It's hard to sever ties with someone who you are comfortable with and who is committing no cardinal sin against the integrity of your union. It seemed illogical for me to throw five years of dating away because our relationship was not *quite* right, especially when no relationship is perfect. Nonetheless, our priorities in life were misaligned.

While I made it a priority to attend midweek and Sunday service with my children, David didn't attend church at all except for the occasional wedding or holiday. It was not uncommon for the kids and I to be dressed and about to leave for church when the doorbell would ring, and David would be standing at the door with an impromptu invitation to go to lunch or dinner. In a seemingly nice gesture, he would try to convince us to blow off church and enjoy a few hours with him.

I wanted someone who had a thirst for the things of God and wholeheartedly desired to serve Him in the house of God with other believers. Although I believe a personal relationship with Jesus and the condition of a person's heart is the most important thing, I lived my life in adherence to the biblical scripture that tells believers "do not forsake the gathering of the saints." The bible compares the body of Christ to a physical body, with many parts (members), each serving a different function. In the book of Ephesians, the apostle Paul, shares how the Body of Christ is composed of diversity of gifts, given by God, to equip his people for service and to fulfill the plans God has. When every part of the body comes together to use their specific gifts, it glorifies God and builds up unity in the body.

I actively tried to live out this calling to glorify God and to teach my children through example. It was difficult being joined to David who did not feel a pull in the same direction. I was also aware that David was teaching my children through example.

Somehow, I had managed to stay on this road to nowhere (or somewhere I wasn't sure I wanted to go) for five years. Perhaps, he was dragging his feet because he had concerns that he couldn't bring himself to say out loud.

Eventually, I found myself at this place in my life where I felt that there had to be a big change for me and my children. I wanted a husband so badly. One particular evening, I prayed and really cried out to the Lord for help. I felt so strongly that the Lord was telling me I had to end this relationship with David and TRUST him. Most of the time I would analyze and dissect inner voice leanings thinking that I would probably figure it all out. But not tonight... it was very clear!!!! So, clear that I knew better than to even question it. I had heard the voice of God deep within me and he had given me a specific instruction.

Almost immediately after I had this encounter, David unexpectedly dropped by my home, and my faith and willingness to trust God was put to the test. As David stood at the door, I cracked the door open a few inches, leaving the door chain still connected, to see and talk to him. He knew if I said something to him it was important.

I said to him, "David, I'm going to tell you something, but you have to promise me in advance that you will not question what I'm saying but will just trust me and do it."

He said, "Ok."

I continued, "I was praying tonight, and I felt the Lord telling me to END this relationship with you. You are never to come by my house again or call me on the phone. I can never see you or be a part of your life."

"Ok," he responded as he turned to walk away.

David made good on his agreement to leave me alone; he never once called me, stopped by my home, or even wrote me a letter. It was as if I was being protected from getting sucked back into a relationship of convenience.

That next Sunday morning, just a day or two after I had severed ties with David, I spotted John, a fellow church goer who I would often see picking up his two small children at the children's church. Every time I would see him, I would say to myself, "GOD, that is the kind of man I want. He loves you and loves his children... and has a job... and so many disciplines in his life." Always after church he left with his kids. I always assumed he was married because he had it all together and it was not uncommon for one parent to pick up children while the other one went to pull the car up to the front.

After church I was told by a good friend of ours that John wasn't married. I said, "I'm going to marry him!!" It was like a revelation of what I felt God had said to me about severing my relationship with David in order for God to move on my prayers for a husband. Just a few weeks later, John's path crossed with mine in a very practical way.

Each year, I would plan a Christmas dinner for about 200 pastors and guests that was very elegant with tight security. Part of planning this event was securing the food menu. The Pastor's wife gave me John's phone number in case I needed any help in the food department. It turns out John was a chef! He helped out so much by providing delicious appetizers for the dinner and he even delivered them. Since I had insisted on planning the event on a volunteer basis, the Pastor's wife took it upon herself to give me something she called a "Love Gift" at the end of the evening. She handed me a beautiful card and inside of it was a gift card to Red Lobster in the amount of $100. That's a lot of food for one person! Since John had also helped out, I told him that I felt like part of the gift belonged to him, so we ended up meeting for dinner at Red Lobster a few days after.

Over the next few weeks, we began getting to know one another and then started dating. Six months after using our gift card, John and I were married, and we became the Brady Bunch. We raised our five kids as brothers and sisters. Life wasn't perfect as no one's life is, but we raised our children in church, and they made Godly choices thereafter. We are so proud of the adults they have become and equally proud of the loving marriage that we are still committed to and enjoy.

After 30 years of marriage, John and I are still in LOVE! I am thankful to God for guiding me and thankful to my mother who taught me a very important life lesson- when you don't know what to do, you TRUST GOD.

Transformation Tip

Be encouraged today. The more I trusted God, the easier it was for me to not let my personal desires, fears and insecurities hold me back from being obedient to his instructions for my life. Once I surrendered MY will for my life and decided to completely trust HIS leading, my actions yielded to God's direction for my life and my life began to reflect his plan. When I fully surrendered to God's Will and entered the territory of uncompromising obedience, I made room for him to move on my behalf in remarkable ways.

My advice to everyone reading this is simple: SURRENDER AND TRUST IN GOD.

Diana Houk was born in Tulsa and raised in Oklahoma. Diana met her husband John in the Children's Ministry of what was then called International Gospel Center. The two were married on June 5th, 1990. John and Diana's marriage brought together a Brady Bunch-style blended family of five children. Diana attended and graduated from RHEMA Bible College graduating in 2000. Diana can be reached at diana_houck@cox.net

5

Defying the Odds

Spoonful of Sugar

By Mike Riddle

Shannon O'Brien Riddle was the most resilient person I have ever met. At one point in her life, she was working to put her husband through law school while in the process of divorcing him and supporting their two daughters financially.

A month later, Shannon was diagnosed with stage 4 breast cancer. She was working in sales at a TV station and had to take time off work for medical tests and treatments. She was told that she was too sick to come back to work as she fought for her life and they cut her medical benefits and disability. So, she had no income, no medical insurance and also lost her family home to foreclosure.

Now she was a single Mom with two little girls, she had no income, no medical benefits, no support and was still battling cancer.

She always said, "We can't control what God sends our way. We can only control how we respond to it." So, she decided to hold her head up, dig deep, and rely on her faith in God. Before her double mastectomy, she had a boobie bye bye party and guests signed her bra.

When she started chemo, she had a hair goodbye party. Her daughters helped shave her head and give her a pink Mohawk. She said, "I'm taking my hair on my terms - not allowing cancer to take it."

That's about the time I met her. We met on eHarmony in February in 2010 and it was a long-distance relationship. She had survived the first bout of cancer and was wearing a wig. She thought I was a surfer boy living at the beach.

She was open, authentic, and shared everything with me. I have never met anyone like Shannon. After a few months, we got engaged.

Those around her, even her closest friends, never saw her cry one tear for herself. She was a warrior and was determined to fight this. After some time, she thought she was in remission and her scans were clear. She was at a concert and was feeling very nauseous with vertigo. She was rushed to the hospital and they determined that she had four cancerous lesions on her brain.

I sat with her at the hospital and we secretly got engaged minutes before she was wheeled into brain surgery. I watched her kiss her girls goodbye, talk over her Will with her Dad and discuss her book with her publisher – she was glowing and smiling. She turned and smiled as she said, "I never knew how much I was loved." That was the gift of cancer for her.

She said, "I've got too much to do. It's not my time yet." Her odds of surviving the surgery were low and, even if she survived, the chances of disability or permanent damage were high. They told her she might not walk again.

She did so well, she was kicked out of the operating area within an hour for talking too much. That's my Shan.

When she was well enough, we were able to get married. Our public engagement came when we went to Disneyland to celebrate her recovery. It was at the Rose Garden at the Disneyland Hotel. Our wedding was beautiful and special. We had a lovely ceremony in Vegas with family and friends. She started a charity to empower people who need assistance in fighting cancer. It is called a Spoonful of Sugar.

She went on to fight cancer five times in a span of three years. She said she always wanted her girls to see her fighting and that she never gave up.

She loved proving doctors wrong. She had such a strong faith and was rarely phased by it. Each time her Doctor asked if she wanted to give up, she said, "I have kids to raise."

Every time she came through something, we went to Disneyland. She always said it's a magical place & there is no cancer there. It's a happy place.

She would do anything it took to try to find a solution. She went to Cancer Treatment Center of America in Tulsa, Oklahoma. She researched options and it gave her the best chance to do it. There, she had a team of doctors who helped make decisions for each patient. She referred to it as the Disneyland of Cancer. They pick you up in a limo.

She was being treated for mastesized cancer that was moving around her body and would manifest somewhere else. She insisted that they remove her ovaries and the doctors said there was no reason to do it and they didn't have any indication that there was cancer there. When they operated, they removed massive cancer in the ovaries. She did a full hysterectomy.

We did fundraisers and raised over $125,000 to help her cover costs to find a cure or give her a different treatment. She would drink a cup of olive oil every day.

She went to Dr. Nezami at Center of Hope. He moved the cancer into her spine so that it would never move again. He helped her so much. She did the hyperbaric chamber and oxygen treatments. He does CTC (circulating tumor cells) and they do a test with a vial of blood. Shannon's was 1,000. He took the cancer out of her body.

It came back in her brain and they gave her a big dose of chemo in her brain. She wanted to visit Nezami to make her body stronger so she could feel better.

She had 25 new tumors in the brain and took medicine to shrink them, did pinpoint radiation.

She did videos for Dr. Nezami and for Kaiser and other organizations to help other people learn from her.

Then she had an infected port and got sepsis. She almost died right then. The Doctor said, "Healthy people don't live through this, much less Stage 4 cancer patients." That was the first time someone took my hope away. But they didn't know Shannon.

After the sepsis, she survived, but her body wasn't really strong enough. We couldn't fight it anymore. She finally lost her battle on February 28, 2015. They gave her six months and she lived five years and seven months.

I didn't know what she was going to go through, but I knew this is where I was meant to be. Her daughters were six and eight. I had never been a Dad. Her ex-husband actually lived with us for a while when he had nowhere to go.

I learned to be compassionate and rarely ever think of myself. Shannon always helped other people even when she was at her sickest.

Doctors threatened to have me arrested or removed from the hospital when they tried to put the breathing tube back in. I told him not to or else it could kill her.

She had divine intervention so many times. I told a nurse; I will punch you in the face if you poke her again. I became her advocate after the first surgery. You MUST be vigilant because other people will make mistakes or try to give them the wrong medicine.

After she passed away, they came to pick her up. She didn't have one bedsore and was very well taken care of. I had never been married nor been a Dad before. It was the greatest adventure of my life.

I have no regrets, other than she is gone.

Transformation Tip

I often saw people fall apart when they were around her. They were scared, sad or even mad. I would tell them, "Shannon knows you are not mad at her: you are mad at the cancer. That's ok." As we all know, no day is promised. For the caregivers, I would say to listen. Stay positive. Be an advocate. The person suffering is right, no matter what. For anyone else who is battling cancer, I would encourage them to remember to focus on living – not just fighting it. Enjoy life and those precious moments that you have.

Mike Riddle *runs a Spoonful of Sugar to honor Shannon and to help other families who are going through cancer. If you would like additional resources or support, he can be reached at Ridd34@gmail.com. To volunteer or make donations, please visit the Spoonful of Sugar Facebook page: https://www.facebook.com/A-Spoonful-Of-Sugar-111267685578019*

The Blind Blogger

By Maxwell Ivey

I grew up in a family of carnival owners. All I ever wanted to do was to take part in the business and eventually own a carnival of my own. However, I was born with retinitis pigmentosa (RP), which meant I would gradually lose my vision. Over the years, I did.

In spite of my fading vision, I achieved the rank of Eagle Scout, graduated from high school and college, and participated in running the family carnival until my dad's death from lung cancer caused our small show to go out of business.

My dad passed away in January, 2003. The day I lost my father, I also lost my best friend. I also lost my business partner, although my family didn't lose the business right away. My younger brother (Patrick), my mom (Patsy), and I kept it going until August of 2006. At that point, we were unable to make our liability insurance payments, so we had no choice but to admit we were through.

My mom decided that we should combine forces with my Uncle Albert's carnival. I was personally against this because we had always competed very bitterly for bookings with my uncle and his family.

I thought to myself at the time, "If we have to lose, why do we have to lose to *them*?" Truthfully, I didn't trust my relatives to give us a fair shake. They had always felt entitled to bookings that we were able to get that they thought should have been theirs.

My uncle wouldn't let me help with the bookings, and my games made less and less money because they just weren't good enough to compete with the options on a good-sized midway.

Seeing how things were headed, my health deteriorated. I was never what you would call healthy. Admittedly, I've always been overweight. When your livelihood depends on moving heavy pieces of equipment, being strong is a good thing.

I put on even more weight and eventually had a health emergency. I was almost kicked out of a motel in Port Lavaca, Texas, for peeing the bed one night. It scared me and my family, so I went to see a doctor.

He said, "Mr. Ivey, if you don't change your life, you aren't going to be around here much longer."

That winter, I found a primary care doctor and asked for her help. She started by putting me on a variety of medicines for high blood pressure, cholesterol, gout, etc. Her first goal was to keep me alive.

After that, she suggested that I might have sleep apnea and pushed me to get tested. I had a sleep study done, which determined that I, indeed, had sleep apnea. In fact, I had an extreme case of it and had probably been dealing with it since adolescence. I was then put on a CPAP machine, so that I would get enough oxygen and get a better sleep at night. The results were amazing. When I started getting a better sleep, I also found I had more energy, a renewed passion, and could think more clearly.

The lessons I've learned from my experiences are why I am always telling other entrepreneurs and those aspiring to start their own businesses how dangerous it is to swap sleep for time invested in your business. You can do it for short stretches, but it's dangerous. Eventually, it will catch up with you and make you even less productive.

After getting that new lease on life, I decided it was finally time to turn my occasional amusement equipment brokering business into a full-time profession. It was time to start something new; something totally my own that I could throw myself into.

Starting an online site to broker amusement equipment in 2008 was extremely challenging. This was before WordPress, Wi-Fi, and social media were mainstream and used by the average Joe in my age bracket. I had to learn so many new things, including how to hand-code HTML, recruit clients, set fees, write copy, build an email list, use social media, record videos, and so much more. I was doing all of that and trying to lose weight at the same time.

In 2012, my doctor convinced me to go to a seminar on gastric surgery. She said, "Max, I know you are trying but you aren't seeing the results you want and need."

I told her I would go but not to get her hopes up because I would probably decide not to go through with the surgery. In all honesty, I viewed the surgery as giving up and admitting I couldn't lose the weight on my own. I also had the idea that gastric surgeries were a quick fix and didn't require any effort.

When I went to the seminar, I learned that only 50% of the people who have such surgeries are successful in losing weight and keeping it off. I was astonished to learn that some people even *gain* weight after a gastric bypass procedure. They told me a bypass only works if you do the hard work to change your lifestyle at the same time. Once I understood that surgery wasn't the "end all, be all," but just one tool in an overall approach, I was in.

On Valentine's Day 2012, I weighed in at 512 pounds. My brother has photos of me where he says I look like I easily weighed more than 600.

Once I decided to get the surgery, I was told I had to first lose 80 pounds, so I did the work. I started drinking more water, changed the portion sizes at meals, started using smaller plates and silverware, switched liquids for solids, gave up caffeine, and got regular exercise. I had my surgery in October 2012.

Thanks to continued hard work, I got down to half my body weight. At one point, my doctor was actually concerned he had removed too much. I finally settled in at around 275 pounds. Of course, I am 6'4, so that is a healthy weight for me.

I continued building my website and growing my business as an amusement ride broker. I wrote blog posts that included images of the rides various carnivals were selling. I shared my experiences on social media, too.

Then something strange happened. People started telling me I was inspiring. I disagreed. I wouldn't say I'm special; I'm just a guy who shows up every day and works his butt off to build a business with the hope of supporting his family.

Eventually, some of my great online friends explained it to me.

Collectively, they said, "Max, here is what makes you inspiring to others. You have a built-in excuse to do nothing with your life. If you wanted to sit on your couch, watch TV (or listen to it) while eating junk food all day, no one would say anything about it. The fact that you have an excuse but choose to show up and take on difficult challenges with joy is what makes you inspiring. There are so many people who *don't* have an excuse, yet they sleepwalk through their lives and do nothing with their time."

I had never considered it that way but realized there was truth in what they were saying. That realization was a *defining moment* for me. So, I decided to embrace the role that my circumstances had given me and actively began to use my story to uplift others.

I started a second website as The Blind Blogger, where I could share my experiences of being an entrepreneur who happens to be blind.

I chose the name The Blind Blogger because people had been calling me that on social media for quite some time. Most people don't know any blind people. That is also true online. I was the only blind blogger active on Facebook and LinkedIn, so the name stuck.

Another good friend challenged me to write a book. I took up the challenge and in January 2014, *Leading You Out of the Darkness Into the Light: A Blind Man's Inspirational Guide to Success* was born.

It wasn't easy. I thought the book wasn't long enough or good enough. I had to be talked into sending it to an editor and getting help sending it out into the world. Thankfully, I had previously met Lorraine Reguly, who helped me through the whole process. With her help, I have since published two additional books that share my experiences and teach critical life lessons.

Since publishing that first book, I won one of Amtrak's 2016 Writers in SResidence awards and took a crazy, solo, once-in-a-lifetime trip across the country, traveling from Houston, Texas, to New York City during the Christmas and New Year's holidays.

I've also done over two hundred podcast and radio interviews. In addition to my amusement brokering business, I now help other creative entrepreneurs promote themselves by booking them on podcasts so they can share their stories, expand their reach, get more publicity for their products and services, and help others.

I've even started sharing my hilarious stories of overcoming my disability, personal setbacks, and disasters through public speaking. I've given talks titled, "Life is Like a River," "Just Press Send—Don't Let Fear

Keep You from Your Dreams," and "Overcoming Adversity and Moving Forward." I've given these talks and others at several national conferences (such as DreamCon and PodFest) as well as at local meetings for top non-profit organizations.

I started my own podcast called *What's your Excuse?* I started that show because so many people have told me they felt inspired after asking themselves, "If Max can do it, then what's my excuse?"

My entire journey *began* after I made the decision to become physically healthy and find a new passion to replace the dream that died when my family's small carnival went out of business. It *progressed*, with my decision to take the necessary, small actions, such as filing for a domain name when I had no clue how to create a website or even if anyone would want to use my services.

It *continues* today, because I continue to say "Yes" when people ask me to try new, bigger, and scarier things. All throughout this process, I have been willing to ask for help and accept help when offered.

Every small step in my journey led to a bigger one, simply because I just continued to face my fears. Now, I'm The Blind Blogger—an internationally known personality.

Looking back, I realize that each opportunity was a steppingstone to where I am today.

I am glad I took each step. Had I not faced my fears and taken actions, I would not be helping people today.

Transformation Tip

Upon reflection, I recognize that my success comes from the following three key pillars, which I have applied—and continue to apply—to my own life:

1) Decide to find solutions, instead of making excuses.

2) Never be afraid to ask for help, or to accept help, when offered.

3) Always seek the positive, in every aspect of life.

The 3rd pillar can be the hardest one because the negative aspects of a situation can sometimes overshadow the positive ones. However, I am here to tell you that something positive can be found in even the most horrific of circumstances. Sometimes, it is simply the fact that the situation is cultivating favorable character traits within you and causing you to grow. For instance, an agonizing struggle with infertility could be cultivating within a person the ability to be content in all seasons.

In my case, my diagnosis with RP taught me how to be adaptable because it required that I release the idea of how I thought my life should be and embrace the reality of what was. In order to make the most of my life, I had to first take ownership of it—the good, the bad, and the ugly.

Most people don't want to hear this, but our most difficult experiences are often a catalyst for character development and refinement and the very story that they will use to impact the lives of others. I am living proof of it.

Known internationally as The Blind Blogger, **Maxwell Ivey** *transformed himself from a morbidly obese, failed carnival owner to a respected equipment broker who is currently in the best health of his life. Encouraged by friends, he started sharing the more personal aspects of being a blind entrepreneur, which led to three self-help novels (www.amazon.com/author/maxwellivey), over 200 podcast interviews, traveling cross-country solo, speaking at national conferences, and starting the What's Your Excuse? Show.*

Maxwell is grateful for all the people who helped and inspired him along the way, so he is determined to pay it forward and help others.
Visit www.midwaymarketplace.com/ to learn about his brokering business and visit www.theblindblogger.net to learn more about his books and the online media publicity services he offers. Connect with him on social media, too.

Out of the Darkness, Retrieving Your Power From Your Past
By Mara Momsen

The shattering of my being and soul began when I was raped at age six. My mother and father got divorced and one of my older brothers decided the way he would handle his pain was to pass it on to me through violence.

I woke up one night to a terrifying situation. I was being sexually assaulted. I remember thinking "If I don't do what I did last time he will know I'm awake." As the encounter progressed, I remember looking at the ceiling. With no thought, my being rushed towards that ceiling and I disappeared into darkness. Except for brief periods of time when visiting with my father in the summertime, I stayed in that darkness for about six years.

When emerging from the darkness around the age of twelve, I soon found myself in another distressing situation. I was being targeted by a pedophile and was being groomed for his pleasure. At that point I had no recollection of the rape that plummeted me into the darkness.

Under duress I finally agreed to have sex with the man. After sex he got angry and called me a liar for not being a virgin. The memories of the earlier rape came flooding into my awareness. During this grooming process, I remember him coercing me into saying that I loved him. I didn't know what love was. As I look back, I can now see how these incidents, and those to come, made me think that sex equaled love. This had made it a challenge to know what a good life partner is. I'm still learning and growing in this regard. I have since understood that rape is an abusive act, not a sexual act.

During the grooming, I was introduced to drugs. I had already tried marijuana a couple of times. He introduced me to LSD, PCP, uppers, animal tranquilizers, etc. I discovered drugs were a great way to turn my emotions off. This ended up developing into a twenty-eight-year addition. After eight years of marijuana and other drugs, I turned to cocaine for ten years, then meth for another ten years. What I came to learn was that the choice of doing drugs that get you up, like cocaine and meth, gives you a false sense of power. This is what I needed to do to survive at that time; it was my coping mechanism.

After breaking it off with the pedophile, I found myself sleeping with older men thinking I could gain love this way. I remember the one time I tried to change my behavior and say no to a guy, I ended up being date raped. Thank goodness that dangerous behavior only went on for a couple of years. At age fifteen or sixteen, I began a relationship with the town's local marijuana dealer and soon moved in with him. I was sixteen and he was twenty-one. I was a wild child, and to this day I wonder why my mom didn't intervene. I believe this is one of the reasons why, until recently, I have never felt loved or worthy.

As I write this all I can think is "that's a lot for a kid to go through".

One thing this crazy journey has taught me is to be resilient. I have always been self-employed and have been a productive person in society. I think one of the hardest times for me was when I stopped doing drugs. I thought that life should have gotten easier, but it didn't.

I lost everything. I was evicted from my home, even though I could prove that I paid my rent. My landlord would not let me get my belongings, so I literally walked away from everything I owned. I lost my business because my dog walking and boarding business was based out of my home. I found myself living in a Ford Explorer with six large dogs. I will never forget the day I was cleaning myself up at a restroom at a park. I looked at my hands and said to myself, "I look like a homeless person." I was in such denial about my situation. If nothing else, I have always been the eternal optimist.

There have been so many *defining moments* on this journey. The one that stands out the most was when my brother, my original abuser, got cancer. When I heard of his illness, I remember hearing the voice in my head state loud and clear "it is now safe to be here on this planet." What I didn't know was that was the moment everything was about to change. Within a month, the desire to do meth dropped away. Even when offered free drugs I had no desire to do them. What this shows me is how powerful our minds are. What I didn't know at the time is that I was being guided by the universe/God/Creator to the next chapter of my life to learn about spirituality, enlightenment and healing.

What I know now is that changing our environment, inner and/or outer, is imperative to changing who we are. Epigenetics shows that our environment plays a big role in our genetic expression and health. A healthy environment enables us to upregulate (health promoting) our genes. And an unhealthy environment aids in the down regulation (health depleting) of genes. I don't know what would have happened if I had not gotten myself out of that dire situation. Being homeless in Los Angeles is not a healthy environment.

I called someone who I had bought two border collies from and asked if they knew anyone who needed a ranch hand. I had to get out of Los Angeles; it was too toxic to me. I was fortunate and three days later I got a call to come work for them. For the next year, I was a goat shepherd in northern California. One of my favorite sayings to this day is "you have never lived until you have spent a month in the middle of San Francisco with eight hundred goats." I worked hard that year, but it was a good year.

I want people to know that it's best to follow your intuition when you get a feeling to do something. Before leaving L.A. I answered an ad on Craigslist for a stress reduction specialist for $100 hour. What I didn't know was that they were selling a Quantum Biofeedback device. Mind you, I had no job and was living in a motorhome at the time.

During the demonstration, I had a feeling come over me and I just started crying. Trust me, this was not like me; I was the tough girl. The one who never let anyone know what I was feeling because it was too dangerous. The device sold for $20,000. Against all odds, I left L.A. with one of those devices and training under my belt. Crazy!!!

This device has taught me about subtle energy and vibration and was another major turning point in my life. My journey has led me down a path to understand that this reality is not what it appears to be. We are more energy than we are matter. This life experience that we call reality is malleable. We are in control of our life and destiny. If you would have told me that back before I got evicted, I would have said you were crazy.

My entire childhood was not negative. I experienced and was exposed to things that have served me in adulthood. My mother was, for lack of a better term, a hippy. So, I learned to meditate when I was very young. Even though I felt that I was neglected, she taught me compassion. There were always people who didn't have families at our house on holidays. All the neighborhood kids would be at our house playing because we had a swimming pool.

My father was a geographer, so I got to travel the world. My grandmother was wealthy and an amazingly strong woman. She lived on a beautiful sprawling country estate in New York and we learned proper etiquette when visiting her. My life has been a wild ride packed with adventure. And there is so much more that I haven't told you about.

By far, the latest chapter of life has been the most enlightening. I realize that if I had not gone through all the experiences, good and bad, I could not appreciate where I am now. I love this dance that I have been dancing with the Divine, God, Creator, The Universe.

This journey has taken me inward. This is where all the answers lie to who and what we really are. We are divine beings having a human experience. We are not broken and never were. We are perfect just the way we are. Self-acceptance is the key to healing.

Do not listen when someone says you are less than or you are doing something wrong. Even if we make a seemingly wrong decision, we are embarking on a path to gain a lesson that we wouldn't otherwise learn. "Wrong decisions" are an opportunity for an awakening; for us to expand in wisdom. There are no wrong decisions, just learning opportunities. Even unwise choices lead us to better ones.

I now find myself in a unique place of understanding that we are all just an expression of all that is, God, Creator, etc. I am embarking on a journey of service. I cannot sit back knowing that I have wisdom to share. I cannot allow others to suffer the way I did in not knowing how beautiful they are when they think they are broken.

We all have wisdom to share. What mess has led you to the message you need to share with the world? Do not be ashamed of your story. Your story has the power to help others.

Transformation Tip

When you find yourself in a place of upheaval or in a transition that you find difficult, just know you will be okay. First of all, breathe. There is a simple breath technique that can help you calm down in the moment. Breathe in to a count of five, hold for a count of five, and exhale to a count of seven. This helps calm the nervous system. Sit calmly for a few minutes and look inward to ask yourself the deep questions. Is this where I want to be in life? How can I make a plan to shift my life? Look for real action steps you can take. And don't be afraid to ask for help. Start meditating.

Inner Child Exercise

Here is an exercise you can do to get in touch with your inner child. Your inner child is the childlike facets of your personality- childlike outlooks, behaviors and coping mechanisms-that developed in childhood and subconsciously surface in difficult situations.

When we have knee jerk reactions to situations, it usually comes from somewhere in our subconscious mind - an old pattern created in childhood to keep us safe. The thing is, it does not serve us as adults to allow the scared inner child to run the show. This exercise should be done every morning for at least a couple of weeks and it only takes 3-5 minutes per day.

Sit quietly and take a couple of deep breaths, eyes closed. Ask your inner child to come sit on your lap. This is not summoning a separate entity from outward or even inside of you. Instead, this is a way to tap into a part of you that you may have locked away. This process brings to your conscious mind any areas of hurt within your subconscious mind that may need healing.

When your inner child comes to the forefront of your mind, look for character traits that might indicate their age. Ask them (that part of you) to share how they are feeling and let them answer without your interruption. You will know what they are saying by looking deep within yourself. The answers are within you. When they are done, thank them for sharing and tell them you love them, and you are here for them and always will be. Let them know that they don't have to worry about the adult issues in life. That is your job. Their job is to play and have fun. In addition, if you have a triggering moment during the day just take a few seconds to remind your inner child that you will be taking care of things and they can go play.

This entire process is a way to reset your mind so that the way you interact with the world will not come from a place of fear and hurt but, wholeness and self-love.

Mara Momsen has been in the healing arts for over thirty-five years and has a never-ending thirst for knowledge. Some of her accomplishments have included earning her degree in body/mind transformational psychology, obtaining certifications in holistic nutrition, hypnotherapy, yoga instruction, quantum biofeedback, Matrix energetics, Re-connective healing, Freedom activation, Havening, life coaching and emergency medicine. Mara also works as a massage therapist and utilizes other technologies such as the Lucia light, heart rate variability, frequency specific microcurrent, Healy and BioWell. Some of her passions are learning about the nature of consciousness, spending time with her dogs, being in nature, and traveling. Mara is currently sharing her knowledge and healing modalities through various courses and private sessions. Mara can be reached via email at <u>maramomsen@gmail.com</u> or at 541-663-6896.

Finding My Summit

By Kimberly Leslie

The very nature of life includes high points and low points. The difference between each of us is the distance between those two extremes and our ability to exist as we climb or fall back on that mountain we call experience. Few are fortunate enough to spend every moment on a warm and comfortable plateau, knowing that today will be like yesterday and tomorrow will be like today. Safe. Warm. Perfect. SWP. The visual of that plateau has been with me since the first time I slipped. I saw that SWP place as my own summit; if I just hung on, I could get there again.

My first serious life crisis occurred shortly after my fifth birthday. I was sitting in a large circle of kindergarten-sized chairs, waiting for the teacher to read a story. Suddenly Charles, the chubbiest little boy in the class, jumped out of his chair and ran straight at me. He kissed me, right on the lips. The chant began almost instantly; "Charles loves Kimberly, Charles loves Kimberly." My little hands covered my ears, but the words continued. I burst into tears and ran the five blocks home.

There it was. The lowest point of my life. We moved shortly after to an idyllic and unspoiled little Florida Gulf Coast town. Harmony. Charles dimmed and the joy of this pristine beach, sunshine and seashells took over. SWP.

Ensuing slides down that mountain and climbs back up became a regularity. Less than two years later, my mother became critically ill. Aunts and uncles came, conversation was mostly whispered, adults hugged me in an entirely different misty-eyed way, and I lived in a down slide aura of fear. Two very long weeks later, I was taken to the hospital and told to look at a second-floor window. There, looking so very small, was my mother, waving to me. As my hand raised to return the wave, I regained my childlike sense of "it's going to be okay."

My teen years passed; most were up, but some were down. Humans are resilient. Long heard phrases like This Too Shall Pass took on meaning. The first death of a grandparent followed shortly by the birth of my first nephew. My father suffering a near life-ending heart attack entailing his need to change to a less physical career, and then unparalleled success with the new family business – so much so that by 17 I had a brand new convertible, private flying lessons, and the reality of college. The icing on the cake was a learned work ethic and inner strength that would define my adulthood.

Just like my mother, just like my father, I was a survivor. I married, had four stair-step children, lost my father, witnessed an initially trusted/hired CEO blatantly steal our thriving family business. I went through a divorce, had my very core threatened by the helplessness of a stranger rape, then learned the ability to again trust over a three-year course of therapy. I reinvented my own career, expanded into related fields, and came out whole and even at a higher place on my inner mountain.

Most of all, I learned that just when we are the weakest, the most helpless, trapped in a previously unfathomable circumstance, the answer is in the ability to bounce, down and up, down and up, as all of those previous lessons had prepared us for. Hope and belief are game changers.

As a business owner, I worked crazy hours. A full-time babysitter provided me the freedom to keep up a schedule that would kill most others. With four ADHD children before the cavalcade of treating medications (or, more importantly, prior to the recognition that ADHD was not only genetic, but was routinely manifested by short attention span, classroom interruptions and impulsiveness), I was often placed in a position of being a single parent called to the principal's office. I would then have to fight the school system and its diagnosis of "emotional impairment" glued to each of my children. Each was extremely intelligent, creative, and capable. The school reports blamed their being "different" on being taught those terrible traits by their single mother who was similarly hyperactive.

We lived in a designer house with a 52-foot built-in pool, a trampoline, the latest in technology (a TRS80 that the family pediatrician said would 'increase eye-hand coordination'), toys, games, lessons, even a pony! We lived a lifestyle that encouraged the then-quirky gifts that the school system considered to be curses imposed by the obvious shortcomings of the mother.

Top of the mountain. An enviable lifestyle, impromptu trips with the kids (Disneyland, a weekend in Toronto to check out the Science Center Museum, Zoos and County Fairs, etc.) But definable tops only exist because bottoms are ever-present. And life can change in a heartbeat.

I'd worked my usual 60-hour M-F week, then had a house party on Saturday evening. On Sunday morning, I woke up very ill with the flu, bronchitis, too sick to move. I spent the day on the couch. The kids, then 11, 10, 9 and 7 fixed their own sandwiches, plied me with orange juice, and behaved. They got up on time Monday morning, dressed, and I drove them to school and then went to my office. By 11 am I'd gone to the Doctor's office, obtained antibiotics, and was back at my desk.

And then the world blew up.

My ten-year-old son, during recess, got into a snowball fight with another boy. The principal put them both at the side of the playground, both hands in the air, on a day where the temperature was in the teens. "Ten minutes!" As soon as the principal walked away, my son bolted. He was actually sitting on a back step of the school, but the principal decided to look for him at my house.

Sometime that morning after we left, our family dog had ripped open the plastic garbage bag from the Saturday night party and made a mess in the front hallway. The window peering principal called CPS ... and the war was on.

The babysitter was stuck in a snowdrift in her driveway and was not there when the kids got home (key under mat), but CPS was. An early 20's caseworker noted five glasses and four plates in the sink, bread on the kitchen counter, unmade beds, the torn bag, and both toilets unflushed with the seats up (boys!) There was also a pile of laundry waiting to be washed. This situation prompted her to determine that the children were in immediate danger and she was going to "save" them by placing them in emergency foster care. I was home within minutes, but powerless against her County Authority.

The kids were crying, screaming; it was like a scene from a horror movie. They were even taken in a police car, when I had always taught them that police were to be trusted. I was really sick but went into what could only be described as Momma Bear mode. Smart Momma Bear. I grabbed a camera and snapped pictures of everything. I had no idea where my children were, and it may well have been the longest night of my life. Their beds still unmade, but no little bodies inside of them. In the morning, the eldest was able to make a phone call after sneaking into the school office when the secretary was outside just before the bell rang. "Where are you? Where did they take you?" I asked. Her answer haunts me to this day. "At school. It was a house." She was crying. "They made us pray last night, saying that this wouldn't have happened if we believed in Jesus." My mouth dropped. "Mom, she wailed, I'm wearing somebody else's clothes. They don't fit …." and the line went dead.

Jesus? My children were the only Jews in the entire school district of six elementary schools. While we were not religious by any means, each went to Sunday School at the local Temple. Each had been taught to respect other religions because we lived in a heavily Christian reformed community that had more churches per capita in the county than anywhere in the entire United States.

Enraged, at everything, I called the caseworker. "You cannot condone making my children pray to Jesus. You cannot condone them being told they would burn in hell if they refused," I said. She wanted to ask questions. "How did you find out?" and then added, "I thought it was best to keep them together." Like that was an excuse.

I'd gone over the edge. Slid down the mountain into an abyss. And I threatened her. "You can't do this in America. I'm going to sue you, the school, the country, your department, everybody." Two hours later, a social worker was dispatched to the school to interview the children; another stranger and in a small room. Alone. I would learn within two days, from my 11-year-old daughter, that it was a bully session. She said, "They tried to get me to say things that weren't true. The lady wouldn't stop. Why, Mom, why?"

The second night, the kids were split up. The girls at one house, the boys at another. The girls were at a house with crosses on all of the walls, but they were not forced to pray. They did have to bow their heads for Grace ("Thank you Jesus...") before they were allowed to eat.

My family attorney was able to get the County to release the children to their father after extracting an agreement that I would have no access to them until a full investigation was completed. Ironically, had they investigated him; they would have learned that he was a cocaine addict. That was one of the many reasons I had filed for the divorce. As the County DSS and their attorneys jockeyed to prove something, anything, my attorney also went to work.

In all, it took 2-3 weeks to get the kids returned. I took them OUT of that school and moved 20 miles to the other side of town. It helped, but there was never any taking back that innocent children had endured the temporary loss of their security and the forcible insertion of terror into their souls. Each was affected, but the oldest had taken it the hardest. Within months, she suffered a complete nervous breakdown, retreating to corners, shaking uncontrollably, and worse.

Little did I know at the time, but our insurance policy had a $100,000 cap on mental illness. A 30-day hospitalization and three psyche visits per week quickly exhausted that and there was no help for those with money. "You own a house," meant I had to sell the house to pay ongoing medical bills. "You own three new cars," meant I had to sell them to pay bills and then buy a replacement on payments. "Oh, your business is worth over a quarter of a million ...." same story. A sick child trumps money.

While the financial hit was devastating, watching the PTSD symptoms in the children was worse. On the day our attorney was ready to file in Federal Court, I got an unwelcome surprise. He showed me the list of those individuals and entities he intended to name – and it was missing the DSS worker who, to that very day, was causing the children to have nightmares, to wake up screaming, over and over. He explained that the worker's husband was a local attorney, a friend of his, and out of deference to his friend, he would not name the wife.

I walked out.

By this time, I had just months until the filing deadline. All but one of the child psychiatrists had told me that my eldest daughter's mind was gone, and she would have to be institutionalized for the rest of her life. One, thankfully, said that the only other option he saw was to move her far away and see if it would possibly help. So, I sold all of my furniture, sold my one remaining half business to my partner, loaded up the station wagon with the kids and the family dog, and pulled a small U-Haul to a faraway state. Poor but safe.

There was no fancy house, no 52-foot pool, but we took the trampoline, some favorite books, just enough clothes, and bits and pieces of our former lives. Our much smaller rented house had a clear view of the mountains. Once the kids were enrolled in schools, I looked from the valley of that mountain to the top and knew I had a job to do. With just over three months to the filing deadline and some overwhelming odds against us, and even though I knew nothing about federal law, I walked into the local law library early on a Monday morning and then lived inside volume after volume looking to teach myself what is surely one of the most difficult areas of law. I was there when they opened the doors and the last one out when it was time to close. There were no computers to search statutes electronically – it was in the 80's. So, I read and read and read. With just days to go, I wrote the pleadings as a pro se litigant, and got them filed just under the wire. I named every damn name/entity on my previous attorney's list ... AND ... the wife of his attorney friend.

Six attorneys had told me that no pro se litigant could last in federal court for even five days. Not even an experienced attorney can beat immunity, they said. It can't be done.

With a clear vision of the mountains always in view, I lasted as a pro se for five years. And I was the first ever to prevail on beating the implied immunity. In the end, they paid. Not enough to make up for stealing four childhoods, but enough to teach us all that wrongs can be righted through determination, work, and a sense of justice being served. The most important win was that we got "injunctive relief", setting case law that will prevent any other family so affected from having to lose in order to win.

Transformation Tip

Different life chapters can often result in different names. So, it is with "Kimberly Leslie." In all, I have had close to a dozen pseudonyms over my career as a writer. It took me many years to put this story into written form, and it's due only to the long view that I now know the intense and lasting effect this experience had on my family. If little else, it came with a valuable life lesson. When you think that you've hit the bottom of a dark and foreboding pit, when there's no juice left in your body or soul, then DIG. You never know what you are capable of until, years later, you look back and see that you did the impossible. You survived.

Kimberly Leslie *has been a prolific writer since she was old enough to write. In her real life, she's a licensed Private Investigator, one who attributes her success to the "Been There, Done That" factor -- plus learning, often the hard way, that to give up is to lose. She can be reached through the publisher of this book -- who will always know where she is.*

6

Hope After Loss

Down the Rabbit's Hole

By Mary Ellen Wasielewski

There are defining moments in our lives, moments that we can recall with surprising accuracy. They can be good moments such as the birth of your first child. However, more often than not, they are ushered in when the world as you know it seems to abruptly end with the impact of having the rug pulled out from under you. These moments precede shock, denial and then a free fall into the darkness of Alice's rabbit hole.

The scream that came from the depths of my soul will never be forgotten - by me or anyone who heard it. I had just taken my boys to visit my parents in Upstate New York, something we enjoyed every summer. My husband, Steve, remained home for work. I had just put my youngest to bed and came downstairs to find my flip phone vibrating across the table. I ignored it, ready to sit on the front porch with my mother and sip a glass of homemade lemonade.

The quiet was again broken by the vibrations of the phone. And then again...

Chapter 5: Hope After Loss

You know that ominous feeling that comes over you? Some people call it intuition, instinct, even gripping fear. *That* foreboding feeling loomed over me as I reached for my phone.

After stuttering the word hello, I heard a woman's voice say, "Please hold for the doctor." I went numb and everything played out in slow motion like a movie scene that I desperately wanted no part of. I couldn't tell you what else was said. I only heard the words *fatal heart attack*. The word *fatal* seared in my mind as I let out a gut wrenching, blood curdling scream- a shriek really. I, along with anyone around, will never forget that ear-piercing sound.

Steve was only 46 years old. He was my rock; the one constant in my life. Yet, in a nanosecond, the life I knew came to a halt. My title as Wife changed to Widow. My children could no longer say "my parents" but would be saying "my (single) mom."

I can remember the smell of the summer July evening, the freshly mowed grass. I can still feel the breeze on my skin. I can still picture my parent's table with their vinyl tablecloth. Sitting at that table was my father with the saddest eyes I had ever seen wanting to fix something that was impossible to fix.

Of all the sights, sounds and smells vying for my attention on that hellish night, the image of my father is by far the most heart-wrenching. To this day, it is branded in my mind and has become a part of me as though I somehow absorbed it into the fabric of my being.

As the initial shock wore off, the grim reality began to emerge. The boys were 13, 15 and 17. College was looming on the horizon, and the recognition of no job, no career, and no husband began to take its toll. I was the main character trapped in a Picasso level picture of stress, anxiety, fear, and grief. If I focused on the fact that my boys were also trapped in this warped scene of destruction and chaos, I would crumble.

While I thought I had prepared for this, I was ill-equipped for the reality. My husband was diagnosed with juvenile diabetes at the age of

13. The battle for the regulation of his blood sugar was frequent, and we were on the losing side often. In his later years, the number of occurrences and the intensity of hypoglycemia increased, as did the multiple car accidents, the ambulance rides and the fear that ensued. Faith was the only thing that kept me going. Faith was the thing that kept us all going. Then came that fateful call, and every cell in my body was in panic.

The life we had imagined had imploded. Rebuilding a new life for the boys and I with such a heavy heart was going to be my greatest challenge. The emotional symptoms of grief were expected. My college psych class discussion of death and dying had equipped me with head knowledge of the 5 stages of grief: denial, anger, bargaining, depression, and acceptance; however, the textbook synopsis fell short from reality. *What about deep yearning, angst, anxiety, and panic? Along with confusion, absent mindedness, irritability, and depression ...*

There were other mental, physical, psychological, and spiritual symptoms that were also missing from the accepted definition.

There is one hard and fast rule when it comes to coping with the death of someone you love and that is that there are no rules. Every death is different, and every relationship is different, so the way each of us experiences loss and grief will be different. Grief is more of a journey than a state of being. When someone dies, those of us who mourn will take that journey in a unique way. It's a journey through some of the most emotionally intense and painful passages of life. It seems as if nothing and no one can help. Oftentimes our only solace is the knowledge that adversity sets the stage for learning and growth. We have to believe that this is true for our own sanity. Luckily- it is.

The most important skills my parents taught were faith and trust. Faith that the Lord will direct my path and trust that He will provide all the tools necessary to climb this mountain in front of me.

God worked though people who chose to be obedient to his promptings and he did it under interesting circumstances. While I was walking on the treadmill, a young man approached me and boldly stated, "If you want help with that problem, meet me here tomorrow at 9:00" then he disappeared like an Irish leprechaun.

I'm not sure if it was curiosity, intrigue or hope that got me to show up. I had questions that I needed answered. *How did he know I had a problem, what was his remedy?*

As it turned out, Jason wasn't a leprechaun- he was a personal trainer, but certainly unlike any I had come across. He said little but encouraged with soft eyes and pushed with a strong calm voice. I couldn't give up. I wouldn't give in to pain. Never before had I worked up such a sweat. He asked for no money. Instead, he instructed me to repeat the same thing every day and, if I had any questions, to come and find him. Before he could leave, I asked him, "Why me?" His response, "Every day I see you here walking that treadmill with tears rolling down your face; I knew I could help."

Most of us have been impacted by sleepless nights at difficult times in our lives. I was no exception having not slept through the night from the day of that life-altering phone call. But that night was different. I slept soundly throughout the night for the first time and woke feeling better than I had in months. The focus was not on the pain in my heart but the pain in my legs from muscles reluctantly brought out of retirement. My teacher had appeared in the form of a stranger and I learned that the chronic stress brought on by grief can be helped when the pharmacy in your own body responds to heart elevating exercise.

Sometime later, while attending church, I was approached by Jack- the agent who sold us our home roughly 20 years prior. He approached me after mass and offered his condolences. He quickly followed up with the question of what my future plans were. Damned if I knew. Jack pleaded, "Come work with me. You will have control over your schedule, your income has no limit, I will train you and I can support you in this difficult time. I'm here today because this is the anniversary of my daughter's death. You see, I know what you're going through."

He was spot on. There were so many times I benefited from the experience of the shared journey through grief, loss, and pain. A secret unspoken language existed. A look of emptiness in my eyes, an aggressive comment to someone, a sigh, the deeper meaning behind these actions was recognized by Jack. I made mistakes and plenty of them. Jack guided, helped, and sometimes took over. For this he received a return on his investment of compassion. By the third year I was the office top producer. We both won. He also received my loyalty and commitment - staying with Jack's firm despite the multiple offers from other companies.

Pay it Forward.

My very wise grandmother used to say the quickest way out of your own hell is to lift someone from theirs.

I began supporting others in grief.

As I had learned in my own pain, most persons grieving- no matter the reason- seem to also suffer with insomnia. I found it was effective to support these fellow travelers on their journey with a 2 a.m. email encouraging them to share their story or as an exercise partner meeting for long walks. Oftentimes just a listening ear was the prescription most warranted.

I would educate them on some of the pitfalls that would come, the symptoms and obstacles. This was a journey I had made and still continue on, as it does not come with a cutoff date. The journey has its own timeline, its own ebb and flow, and each journey is different. I provided a flashlight, a compass, and a map, but they needed to do the work and take the journey. This is the trip of 1,000 miles and they had to begin with that single step.

There are moments in our life that define us, but often in ways that we don't expect. I have walked the long journey from the end of life as I knew it, through the dark rabbit hole and emerged on the other side with a new beginning. My husband's death was the *defining moment* that set this journey

Chapter 5: Hope After Loss

in motion. With guides and teachers, I discovered what a transition could be and what it could do. I firmly believe that all transitions have a purpose.

The merger of all my experiences gave me a perspective that honored both the art and science of transitions. While my experiences gave me a point of reference that I would not wish on anyone, I had survived the unfathomable and my uphill battle had created a foundation within me that had been tested and tried.

I became a completely different person. Things that began with one context, suddenly found their true potential in a different context. Sometimes we must endure the unthinkable to reach our highest expression of self.

Only God knows who we are *truly* called to be. That is why it is so important to trust Him. When we truly trust Him, we are not afraid of change because we know that change is there to serve us so that we can evolve to our purest form of self.

Change is a constant factor of life and it gives way to possibilities. My road began with a change that happened *to* me. Then subsequent changes occurred *because* of me and because of the obedience of others. I transformed *because* I surrendered to the journey. My journey.

And walking my journey was difficult.

It is extremely hard work- the path to healing. We must heal emotionally, mentally, physically, and spiritually in order to survive. Even so, I wanted more than to survive...I wanted to thrive! So, the work did not stop with a new job, but continued on as I reset my life by redefining my purpose, recalibrating my vision of using my gifts, talents, and experiences to serve others.

I continue to follow my Grandmother's advice on a larger scale by helping individuals and organizations through their struggles with life-altering transitions.

DEFINING MOMENTS SOS (Stories of Survival)

Transformation Tip

We have in us the ability to be resilient. To be knocked down seven times and get up eight. It does take courage, persistence, and perseverance. Our journey can be made easier with guides; those who are survivors can make the depth of the rabbit hole shallower. Faith does not mean your journey will be easy, it does however make it possible. If possible, seek out others who have walked a similar journey and be a guide to those who are embarking on a path similar to yours.

Mary Ellen Wasielewski *is the Founder and CEO of BLT Strategies, Executive and personal crisis coaching. Her team helps individuals and organizations remain productive, engaged, and healthy during times of adversity. Turn your chaos and pain into purpose while rebuilding. Your story isn't over, it's just the Next Chapter.*

Mary Ellen can be reached at 617-340-9548 or via email: Maryellen@bltstrategies.com. For more info, visit BLTStrategies.com.

Perceive to Achieve

By Neal Hooper

I grew up as one of five kids to a single mother with clinical depression. Things were hard financially and emotionally growing up. In spite of that (and possibly *because* of that) I grew close to my mother in my early years. Against all odds, I went to college and found success with no support from home. I struggled but came out on top in most of my endeavors.

In 2013, I began dating a girl and even got engaged to her later that same year. We had a ton of fun together and had an amazing courtship which involved concerts, hikes, and boating trips.

Shortly after we got engaged, I was offered a full-time job as Director of Internal Communications and Student Leadership at a Business College in Salt Lake City. Things seemed to be going very well for me and the future was looking bright.

Throughout our courtship, I noticed that little problems started getting bigger. We did not see eye to eye on things like communication, parenthood, and family values. Moreover, our professional and familial aspirations were conflicting, and we were having difficulty reconciling our differences. I began to realize that no matter how many times we tried working through them, these things were getting harder to ignore and that we were slowly growing apart.

Emotional needs of mine were unfulfilled, and it seemed that she was unhappy about key parts of our relationship as well. I began to believe that our relationship was as though I was an emotional scuba diver longing for the deep sea discoveries of life while she was happy snorkeling among life's coral reefs. My level of depth and curiosity seemed to be too much for her.

I ultimately realized that we would not be happy together in marriage and was now faced with the cruel decision of continuing in the relationship in spite of these concerns or walking away from it and cutting our losses.

Shortly after having this troubling realization I began my new Director role which was very demanding. I was put in charge of new student orientation and tasked with completely overhauling the student leadership structure and peer mentor programs.

In the midst of navigating a demanding career and relational turbulence with my fiancée, my mother was diagnosed with stage 4 cancer and given four months to live.

In one of the most uncertain and vulnerable periods of my life, I decided to rip the band aid off and cancel the wedding. Just three months later, my mother passed away. The pressure from a new and demanding career, coupled with the pain and emptiness that comes from a failed engagement and the grief of losing my mother was almost unbearable. This entire time period was one of the darkest times of my life. Any one of those events in isolation would have been challenging but having to face them all at once was soul crushing.

In that season of darkness and despair, I knew I had a decision to make. I could look up and out, or down and in. I'm eternally grateful that I made the difficult decision to look heavenward rather than to the numbing and destructive behaviors that would have permanently derailed my life. I entered a season of soul searching and discovery. I realized that my life had completely fallen apart and that this was an opportunity to think deeper about where I wanted to go and what I genuinely wanted out of my life.

I drove all night through the Utah desert and played my Hawaiian ukulele into the night. At sunrise I went to the great salt flats and walked by the shoreline. I was the only soul in sight. There on the pure white salt with no sound except the gentle wash of the tide, I had a one-on-one conversation with God. This was a *defining moment* for me. I committed to rebuilding my life, to becoming the best version of myself, and to reaching for the stars.

On my way home from that experience, I remembered a video I saw in high school about vision boards and life mapping. I decided to take action and make my very own vision board. I got very strategic about the direction I wanted my life to take. I looked deep into my soul and articulated the things that excited me. I then found images that represented those things.

I compiled the images into a collage and put it everywhere. I printed it out and put it on the front of a binder. I made a digital version and even made it the lock screen on my phone. It was on my wall in the bathroom, and as I looked at it every morning and every night something extraordinary began taking place. I not only began perceiving value in these beautiful visuals, but also capability in my skills and resources to achieve them.

So, what were the images that inspired me most? 1.) a photo of me and Jesus embracing at the gates of Heaven and 2.) a photo of a couple on the beach holding each other up and spinning on the sand in the setting sun. Several times per day, I would look intently at these pictures with

Chapter 5: Hope After Loss

anticipation that my life would one day reflect them. I became excited, expectant, and determined.

My life completely turned around in the years that followed. A mere three years later, I was humbled to witness the manifestation of one of the images on my vision board. Life had been going well for quite some time. I was excelling in my career and had married a kind and beautiful woman.

While visiting family in California, we stopped at the beach for an afternoon of leisure. In a moment of spontaneity and love, I picked up my wife and twirled her in the air above me. At that very moment I remembered one of the images on my vision board...I was living out that exact image. I know that my life changed because I took the time to really articulate my dreams and made the necessary changes to passionately pursue them.

Transformation Tip

In these moments of hardship, there are two versions of yourself grasping for the driver's wheel of life: strong you and weak you. It is absolutely crucial to let strong you take the wheel before weak you gets in the driver's seat. Weak you wants to numb the pain, indulge in destructive behavior, and ultimately take the path of least resistance (and joy). Strong you is intentional, desiring to rebuild, and ultimately thinking about

Long-term value and outcomes. Letting strong you take the wheel will allow you to become the architect of your life and seize the opportunity to rebuild it from the ground up.

We know it's important to take our time to plan vacations, projects, or even weddings, but we rarely take the time and effort necessary to plan our lives. Why not become a travel planner for your life and articulate where you want to go and what you want to see and experience along the way? You have to map out your life and clearly articulate *what* you want and *why* you want it, but this is not something that weak you wants to do. In these crucial moments of hardship and trial, as hard as it may be, you must make the conscious choice to give strong you decision power and rebuild your life. This is how you turn tragedies into defining moments of strength.

Neal Hopper's story is one of grit and passion. He went from cleaning storage units at age 13 to support his family, to earning a double master's degree and joining a fortune 100 company, to now building an empire of growth and passion. He's the product of loving mentors, chance-takers, and lots of faith. Neal is the creator of "the Perceive to Achieve" framework, an effective life mapping and goal setting system that empowers you to articulate your goals, and confidently pursue them.

Neal is married to his soul mate and better half, Aubrea Hooper, and together they have three beautiful children. Aside from hiking, playing the guitar, and creating beautiful things, he loves helping people reach higher and love deeper...and pineapple.

Neal would love to get to know you better and have you join his community of achievers. Find more information about the Perceive to Achieve framework and how you can level up at https://www.perceive2achieve.com or email Neal directly at neal@perceive2achieve.com

Dark Effect of Suicide

By Hannah Brown

Imagine a hole. A hole you're thrown into.

You go, flailing, fighting against gravity but unable to grasp anything to slow or stop your fall.

You went without your permission, control or consent.

You didn't trip, stumble or even step somewhere you shouldn't have; it appeared and swallowed you up.

The hole is so dark you see nothing, not even your dreams, hopes, not even your future.

Chapter 5: Hope After Loss

This is what it feels like to lose a child.

You tumble headfirst into something so dark, so foreign that you hardly recognize your own reflection in the mirror.

The hole is only big enough for one person, so you are not only plunged into a dark, unfamiliar world; you're there alone.

The feeling of separation from everyone else, no matter how hard you cry out for someone, anyone to hear you and pull you out of the hole; silence. No response.

You feel a true, palpable panic once the numbness subsides. Once reality sets in and you begin to see your situation for what it is, your biggest fear in the world has come true; one of your children is dead.

The worst, most horrific loss a parent can face has just become a reality, YOUR reality. You are forever changed; your life as you knew it will never be the same.

The darkness surrounding you in this hole that you now exist in seems unending.

But I'm here to tell you, if you look up you can see a light. The tiniest speck of it penetrates the hole you lie in.

You don't notice it at first, you think your eyes are playing tricks on you.

It doesn't help you see anything at the bottom of the pitch black pit, yet you know it's there.

You know in your heart you are not alone.

I struggle every minute of every day to see this speck of light; but I do catch a glimpse of it now and then.

When I look at and talk to my other two wonderful children. When I see them and the amazing things they have done in their lives, the adversity they have overcome and how truly magnificent they are.

When I look into the eyes of my beautiful grandchildren and witness their innocence or hear their laughter.

These are only a few of the things I see in that pinhole of light darting into the hole.

These are enough.

Because I know one day, even without Sam here, that speck of light will eventually, slowly, get just a little bit bigger.

There will be brighter days ahead, days filled with more laughter.

I'll always be in the bottom of the hole; I've accepted this as my truth. It's my life now and as gut wrenching as it is, I know that by accepting this as my home, it will help me to help another parent.

I can be some sort of refuge to a mother or father who has just fallen into their own nightmarish hole.

I can BE that faint speck at the top of their hole; that glimmer that they aren't sure they saw.

But they will see it, just as I have, they will; I'll make sure of it.

Transformation Tip

To parents,

My strongest piece of advice to you is this- don't be afraid of the grief. Stop battling, surrender to it. You must go through it to get to the other side.

Secondly, NEVER be afraid to talk about your deceased child. They matter as much in death as they did in life. Keep their memory alive; because if you don't, who will?

Hannah Brown lives with her husband in Missouri. She has two surviving children and two grandchildren. She is a Suicide Prevention advocate and public speaker who enjoys writing poetry, painting, all genres of music and visiting her home state of Texas. Hannah can be reached via email at: hannahs69@icloud.com

Dying to Live
By Linda Espinoza

We were in year four of my husband Salami's diagnosis with ALS (aka Lou Gehrig's Disease). My kids and I were struggling with all the lifting we had been doing in the years prior. Not to mention the emotional pain. Salami was still using his walker, but it was getting scary because he could only stand up to hold on for transfers. His body was rapidly betraying him, and the paralysis was robbing him of the ability to stand up straight, leaving him hunched over. Showering him had become a nightmare, as we didn't have a handicapped shower at the time, and he was still close to his 250 lb. weight from when we began our journey.

The daily caregiving needs required us to do everything for him, but the hardest of all was trying to understand what he wanted to communicate. We were left to be his voice but didn't always know what he needed. It had all become so exhausting and beyond overwhelming for us but losing his voice was, for him and for us, the biggest blow.

One day I was feeling incredibly sad and depressed. Fatty, as I called him, was laying back in his lift chair which had become his bed for the last 3-4 years. As I stood over him, I asked, "Do you ever ask *why*? Why did this happen to you?" Surprisingly, he told me, "No, I never ask why because I'm grateful for the years I had with our kids as they were growing up... and I'm grateful that this didn't happen when they were young." He continued, "There's nothing I can do about it...it is what it is."

Here I was crying and feeling sorry for us, thinking of all we had lost, and all we would never have. Yet, my Fatty who had this horrific terminal disease was... grateful?

Why was I not having the same experience?

It was then that I experienced my *defining moment* and my perspective shifted instantly. I wiped my tears and said, "You're right, you're right!"

I realized then that we had been waiting for death to knock on our door. We had been so focused on the 2-5 year prognosis given to us by the doctors that we had allowed it to rob us of joy and the life we had been gifted by our creator whom I call Papa God. We had been so focused on his inevitable death, that we had forgotten to enjoy the life he had left.

Everything changed *that* day because I changed. I changed the way I looked at our lives and how we would move forward living with ALS. I told my Fatty, "We're gonna start dying to live, instead of living to die."

In a prior conversation with my eldest son Markus, he told me that Marcel, my youngest child, had gotten the short end of the stick because he was still in high school and, unlike all the years we attended all three of our kid's sports and activities, that year we missed a lot of everything. We'd go to bed late and wake up late.

The daily care was overwhelming and exhausting. I had no drive or energy to live and enjoy life anymore. I felt a part of me was dying a little each day, along with my husband. While I was aware of this, I hadn't been able to break through the barriers that were standing in my way, until I had these two conversations with Salami and Markus. I believe the reason for that was because my WHY wasn't big enough, Living hadn't become BIG ENOUGH.

So, what did I do?

I realized that, while it wasn't fair that ALS had come and interrupted our lives, I had a choice to make in how it would play out.

ALS had messed with my family, my children, and my love for life. That was enough for me to say, "No! You don't get to be the boss! I serve a God that is greater than ALS!"

Recognizing that God is sovereign, I decided to focus less on our trials and more on the lesson that He wanted me to learn through them. I asked

Chapter 5: Hope After Loss

myself, "How is God using this situation to glorify Him...to make us stronger?"

The first thing I did was make it clear to my Fatty that, while he had ALS, ALS didn't have us. I took a stand and held on to the promises of God... Beauty for Ashes. Period!

I let Fatty know that we would be attending everything Marcel, Markus and Maryssa had going on at school and in their lives. I told him, "I don't care if they just announce Marcel's name, we're gonna be there." And we were. I was committed to the change. I resolved to leave a legacy of triumph over tragedy.

I wanted my kids to remember that their father was still a whole person and that they could still make beautiful memories with him. I became like Wonder Woman; determined to reveal the true warrior that exists within each one of us, if we're willing to let him/her out. Not only for them, but also for Fatty and I.

As I told Salami what my plan was for our new life, he seemed relieved. As if he was waiting for one of us to have enough courage to take a stand. He knew I was serious when I told him, "I'm not waiting for death to come, I want to live and, if you want to do this with me, then we will. If you don't, I'm doing it anyway." I was no longer willing to compromise my own happiness because neither one of us knew how to fix the brokenness in our lives.

I even told him if he didn't want this then I'd get someone to help care for him if I had to. At that point and to the end of his life, I was his full-time, 24/7 caregiver and wife. Happily, he agreed to go on the journey of a lifetime with me. In sickness and in health.

From then on, I got straps for our van. A van that helped change our lives and was given to us by a beautiful, kind couple in our community of Firebaugh, California. At the time, we hadn't used it because Salami still wanted his independence and wanted to continue using his beloved Chevy pickup and his scooter, instead of his powerchair. The only bad thing, I was having to lift him and break down the 100-pound scooter every time we'd go anywhere.

I had to be the change I wanted to see. We began to use the van and the power chair from that time on. It was life transforming! I cried the first time we went to our first doctor appointment because this gave us the chance to start over. This was me living in my prayers.

We started going to church every week. That was non-negotiable. I was also more committed to my journaling...it's what kept me sane. We began going to the movies and lunch with our very dear ALS friends. We began attending Giants baseball games and hanging out with family and friends more. We began walking in our precious little town of Firebaugh. That became one of my most powerful forms of selfcare which I now call prayer walking. It's where I circled the town in prayer.

Fatty also rode on his own around the block when he needed time alone. I highly recommend it to anyone who is struggling to hear God's voice, or even your own. It's not magical, but I can almost bet you in time, you'll see a miracle.

Sunday dinners were critical to my life support. I never realized how powerful the simple act of gathering around the table with those you love can be. I had always done that with our own children, but this was with "Our Crew" as I called my intimate circle, who were also our lifeline.

I'm eternally grateful to "Our Crew" which consisted of my mama, my two sisters (Carmen & Alice) and their families, my brother-in-law Michael, my nephew Michael, and his family. And of course, my own children and grandchild Milania. Sunday dinners became an intentional act of saying I can be the change I want to see in my own life. We looked forward to Sunday dinners and Salami loved them!

In my family we love gatherings, food, and music. While there was always laughter and joking, the music is what still plays on in my mind. I'm reminded through music that, though the song may end, the music will last forever. Our Crew will never know how crucial they were to our survival.

On January 25, 2018, my husband Salome Espinoza took his walk into eternity with Jesus. I'd like to believe, as my friend Melanie once told me, that I walked him to the gates of heaven. When he passed, he was surrounded by me, our children and granddaughter...plus a home filled with his closest family and friends. There were many miracles that happened during the transition time. I wish I could share it all with you here, but that's a story for another book, which I intend to write.

Our story is proof that we can overcome anything when we make our mind up to do so. Truth be told, fear has been a factor in my life for far too long. Not really any specific fear; just fear of fear. But, when I became a fully surrendered believer in Jesus Christ, I realized that fear can't walk on the same path as faith; fear must bow down to faith.

I'm an overcomer because of what God did in my life, not the other way around. I give Him all the glory for my story. The pen is in His hand and I couldn't be happier.

Today, after enduring seven years of living with ALS and grieving the loss of my husband for nearly three years, I am at a place of *peace*. I am finally pursuing my dreams and becoming the woman I believe I was created to be. It has not been an easy road but, what I know for sure is, there is always hope. It exists within us all.

Be willing to find your spark of hope... it might just create a wildfire of belief in yourself and enable you to become who God created you to be.

Transformation Tip

Have you ever hit rock bottom and struggled to find hope? Have you ever been in a storm so great you felt it had come to stay? Can I tell you, that's not your truth. Just like when Jesus calmed the storm for His disciples in the gospel of Mark (Mark 4:35-41), he can do the same for you. He cares for you and he cares about the things you're going through. He wants to guide you in trusting Him for the answers you seek. Be willing to open your heart to Him and see how he changes your entire life - just like he did mine.

Your life may look a mess today but trust me- it's your mess that will create your message. Seek Jesus. He is the answer.

For anyone that needs a connection to find the hope I speak of, I am a lover of the table, it's where I feel the most connected and where I believe true connections are made. I would love to share my table with you.

I would be honored to help encourage and support you on your own Jericho Miracle.

Linda Espinoza *lives in Central California and is finalizing her book,* Tell Your Heart to Beat Again: How Your Brokenness Becomes Your Breakthrough. *Please feel free to email her at* lindaespn@outlook.com.

7

Daring Escapes

I Survived Human Trafficking

By Debra Rush

On a cold February night in 1999, I met a man who promised me the world. "Girl, you're beautiful," he said. I ate up his flattery. My insecurity and the need to feel good about myself made me a perfect mark.

He inquired, "What do you want in life?"

"I want to go to school and make something of myself."

"Those are big dreams, girl."

He took me to breakfast a few weeks later and hit me with a proposition. "I can tell you how you can make $25,000 in just a couple of weeks."

"How can I do that?"

"Let me take you to Los Angles. There is a need for escorts. You'll date men who will take you to dinner, a party, or the theater." His voice raised. "You're gorgeous, girl. Every man will want to have you on his arm."

"That's all?" I trusted him. After all, he had given me his full and undivided attention.

Two days later, I sat in his car on our way to Los Angeles. Shortly upon arriving at our hotel, the demon in him came out. That night, he beat me for the first time. But it wasn't the last.

Over the next ten months, I obediently did as I was told. However, there were times I tried to escape. A beating that left me bruised, with missing teeth, and in bed recovering for a week. My only goal was to survive. The times I tried to leave, he found me. Finally, with the help of a "date", I managed to escape and find a safe place, which was the Fresno County Jail. After my release from jail, Daddy, my biological father, took me to a safe place with relatives in Sacramento.

Unfortunately, at that time, no avenue or efforts were in place to expose human trafficking, and there were limited resources available to help me cope with the specific trauma I had endured. Although I was in a safe physical location, I had no tools for healing. I didn't even realize that I had been trafficked. I had been set free physically but was still in emotional bondage. My nightmare had just begun. Over the next eight years, I suffered from what I now know as Post Traumatic Stress Disorder (PTSD).

Drugs, sex, pregnancies, and running from the law became my life. I lived in fear of my pimp finding me. I lived in fear of drug dealers or losing my kids. I lived in fear of the police.

During those years, my daddy was the one person I could always count on to be there for me. He never failed to rescue me. On Christmas night, 2008, that all changed.

The police were on my trail. I had failed to follow court orders, and it was a matter of time. I pulled into a gas station. Sirens lit up behind me and an officer pulled me out of my car. "I got you," he said. "I've been looking for you."

Strangely, on Christmas night, the holding cell stood empty. It usually held too many women to count but, this time, I was alone. I immediately picked up the phone to call the one person that wouldn't let me down, my daddy.

"Daddy, I've been arrested."

He didn't say anything, just listened until I finished. After a long pause, he said, "Debbie, I love you so much, but I can't do this anymore. I'm going to tell you this one time. I'm not coming to see you. I'm not putting money on your books. You're going to have to figure this out on your own. Don't call the house. Don't call me."

Without giving me a chance to respond, my daddy, my hero, the man I could always count on, hung up.

Did I hear correctly? My daddy wouldn't abandon me. I called back. No one answered. I tried several times. There must be something wrong with this phone.

"Officer, this phone isn't working."

"It's working."

After I hung up, the full realization that Daddy had rejected me hit me. Clutching my chest, I let myself fall to the floor, pulling my knees to my chin. I suddenly felt so embarrassed of the ugly person staring back at me, reflected on the bars of the cell. What had I become?

Somewhere deep within, something began to stir—a cry of the heart—a feeling of profound aloneness. I sat alone for three and a half hours pouring out my soul to the one person Grandma taught me would listen.

After rejecting God for so many years, would He still be willing to listen? Would He care? No person in the world wanted me. God must hate me, too. How could God, in any way, look down from His mighty throne and see this wretched person I had become and want to do anything for me? How could He care?

There was no other choice. I had to try. This was a *defining moment* for me.

In my spirit, I cried out. *Lord, Lord, please just look at me.* Over and over, I heard a cry inside of me. For the first time in my life, I knew I wasn't going to fix this. Only one could, and that was God.

I prayed, "God, if there is any possibility that you're still listening to me, please take me back."

A commanding presence overtook me and occupied the room. A wave of emotion flooded my mind. Uncontrolled tears surged forth. I sat in that cell alone, crying, praying, pleading with God. When I was abducted, it wasn't my fault. But the decisions made over the last eight years were entirely my own. "I did that," I confessed out loud. "God, whatever you want to do to me, I deserve." After praying, I sensed that everything was going to be alright. I fell into a deep, peaceful sleep.

I knew Daddy meant what he said. He wasn't coming to see me. When I woke up on December 26th, I knew I had to change my life.

Mercifully, the judge gave me a few months in jail instead of sending me to prison. I served my time and went home with a changed attitude.

Over the next two years, with the help of some incredible mentors, I began to put my life in order. In October of 2010, I attended a Christian women's conference. After attending a workshop promoted as HUMAN TRAFFICKING, I realized then that I had been a victim. The next day, alone in the woods, I felt God calling me to go out into the streets and rescue my friends who were still out there. But I wondered how that would happen.

Through a series of Divine appointments, I met Tiffany Apodaca. We co-founded **Breaking the Chains**, an organization dedicated to rescuing and rehabilitating human trafficking victims. With the support of law enforcement and the community, we have opened offices, training facilities, and a safe home. It is only because of God that I stand today healed and whole. I am grateful to be living a life of purpose and to be able to take part in someone else's story of healing.

Chapter 6: Daring Escapes

Transformation Tip

Know the Red Flags of a Sex Traffic Victim

- Evidence of being controlled
- Not free to leave or come and go as she/he wishes
- Responds with rehearsed answers
- Lacks control of earned money or identification
- Avoids eye contact
- Defensive or argumentative
- Mistrust of individuals displaying compassion
- Bonded with her/his abuser, despite physical or sexual violence
- Tattoos or scarring of trafficker's name and/or symbols on the victim's body
- Visible signs of sexual violence, physical restraint, confinement, or torture
- Malnourished, exhausted, sleep deprived
- Poor hygiene

If you suspect someone is being trafficked, contact 1-888-373-7888. Resource: YWCA

Debra Rush is the Founder and CEO of Breaking the Chains. Her insight and experience into this daunting industry is the driving force behind Breaking the Chains' founding. Debra, too, is a survivor of human trafficking. Debra, who has a degree in Human Services, works closely with the Fresno Police Department's Trafficking Task Force. She is an alcohol and drug counselor and a national trauma expert. A proud alumnus of the Fresno Chamber of Commerce's Leadership Fresno Class XXXIII (33), Debra has gained notoriety as a passionate community leader. She humbly holds the title 2018 California State Woman of the Year and is a published author. Although she has accomplished much since her transformation, Debra's most cherished achievement is being the proud wife of Mark Rush and the doting mother of seven beautiful children.

Read Debra Rush's entire inspirational and life changing story in her book A Cry of the Heart: Human Trafficking, One Survivor's True Story—by Debra Rush with

Penelope Childers. Available wherever books are sold. Her true story proves no one is beyond redemption. Journey with Debra from despair to success and find a reason to hope. For more information on Breaking the Chains, email Debra@btcfresno.org or visit www.btcfresno.org.

Lost

By John Warner

In August 1952, I was an Eagle Scout with Troop 80 of the First Methodist Church in Pampa, Texas. At 16, I was the oldest boy in the troop and was a Junior Assistant Scoutmaster. Our troop sold hamburgers and soft drinks at the Top O' Texas Rodeo each summer. With the money we made, we would camp out for a week at the Cuchara Campgrounds in the Colorado Rocky Mountains near Blue Lake and the Spanish Peaks.

West Spanish Peak stood 13,626 high and was the larger of the Spanish Peaks. Our troop accepted the challenge that summer, drove in our Scout bus to the base of the mountain and began the climb.

I came prepared. I had a canteen of water and six small boxes of raisins around my waist. After climbing a few hours, we made it past the timber line and could soon see the top. At the top, I shared my raisins with the other guys in the troop.

When it was time to start back down, I stayed behind to tie my canteen and the empty raisin boxes on my hip so they would not interfere with my descent. When I started down, I was surprised that I could not see any of the troop.

"Where is everybody...everybody...everybody?" I called out. My voice echoed down the mountain.

"Over here...over here...over here." Came an answer seemingly from my left.

I thought that was strange because we did not climb up that way. But I headed to my left, climbing down quickly to catch up to the rest of the troop.

"Wait for me...me...me." My voice again echoed down the mountain.

"Wait for Scooter (my nickname)...Scooter...Scooter," came the reply still further to my left.

When I hit the timber line, I still had not caught up to the rest of the troop. I decided that I had been fooled by the echoes and began circling to my right to find the trail that led back to our bus.

By this time, it was beginning to get late. Just before dark, I stepped in a creek and got my feet wet. Ultimately, I did not find the rest of the troop. Defeated, I made a bed from leaves and curled up on the ground.

I spent the night on the mountain - tired, cold, and scared

The next morning, I started out again and found no sign of our troop. I was discouraged. I had no idea where I was. I had no idea if I would ever find my way back. Suddenly, I looked up in the sky and shouted, "Okay, God, get me out of this and I'll be a preacher!"

I expected to feel exhilarated by this proclamation. Instead, I felt nothing. That was the biggest let down I have ever experienced! It was as if God said to me, "Do you think if I wanted you to be a preacher, that I would scare you into it?" As I walked along, I thought about a sermon I had heard where the theme was, "The World Needs More Christian Truck Drivers." Since I had determined at that very moment that I was not going to be a preacher, I decided that I would try to be the best Christian I could be at whatever vocation or profession I ultimately wound up following.

As I contemplated my future, I found a paved road and hoped it would lead me to civilization. I kept walking. Through the trees I saw a lady on horseback. I hoped that she could give me directions. In a few seconds I was looking up at her. "Ma'am," I said. "Can you tell me if there is another road up there?" She looked at me thoughtfully.

"There sure is," she replied. "I've been looking for you!"

"For me?" I thought. She went on to explain that about 200 residents of that area were looking for me and that about once a week during the summer they took the time to search for a different wanderer. This week, they found themselves looking for a kid from Pampa, Texas, that they did not even know! Her name was Diane Tessitor. She was the wife of a local postmaster.

I piled on the back of her horse. She took me in to Laveta, Colorado, from where I ultimately was reunited with my troop. My Scoutmaster was very upset with me. He put me in a car and sent me home immediately.

It was early the next morning when I got home. When I arrived, I found the house empty. I went straight to bed.

My parents and my sisters were at a friend's house that night before and did not get home until very early that same morning.

They picked up the Sunday paper on their way into the house. My picture was on the front page with a story about how I was missing in Colorado. Nobody had thought to call them. Or if they had tried, then there was no answer. I woke up to quite a commotion in our living room!

My sister, Karen, came into my room. I heard her say, "He's not lost. He's asleep in his bed!"

Needless to say, I had some explaining to do.

Later my dad summed up my experience by saying, "Only in America would one kid be so important that 200 people cared enough to take time out of their lives to look for him." I agree. I will be forever grateful to the other 199 whom I never met and who regularly looked for lost souls like I was.

We, indeed, live in a great country!

Chapter 6: Daring Escapes

Transformation Tip

When I found myself "lost", I remembered a particularly important lesson that I learned in Boy Scout training- people who are lost often go in circles. Knowing this, I made it a point to keep going in a straight line until I reached a road. Then I followed that road.

This lesson can be applied to everyday life as well. It's so easy to get caught up in the self-defeating cycle of just doing what we have always done and start "going in circles". If you find yourself circling the same mountain in life, be willing to reevaluate your options to assess if there is a different and more productive way that you can approach the given situation. Sometimes a change in perspective is all you need to "go in a straight line" from where you are to where you want to be.

John Warner *has practiced law in Pampa, Texas, since 1962. He and his wife, Judy, have four children and nine living grandchildren. He taught a youth Sunday School Class in the First United Methodist Church in Pampa for 50 years. He has been an Optimist baseball coach for 11-12 year old boys since 1974. He has been the chair for more than 100 civic projects in Pampa. He can be reached at* jww_pampa@yahoo.com

---

My American Dream
By Eli Sotelo

At birth, I was among the disadvantaged whose mother could not afford to deliver in a hospital. She birthed me in our family's home in Acapulco underneath the kitchen table with no medical assistance. As an infant, I had health complications that terrified my mother; my eyes would bleed when I cried, and she would often awaken to the sound of me gasping for breath.

When I was two, my mother took me to a substandard medical clinic and despite no clear diagnosis for my eye bleeding and soft skull, the doctor said I had bronchitis and may not survive. She went home brokenhearted.

My father had a habit of chasing women who were not his wife. It started off discretely but progressed to brazen and continuous affairs. His work would often take him out of town, so he secured a woman in each town to keep him occupied. Although my father made good money, he had a habit of squandering it on less than noble vices. When he was not spending on himself, he made sure to pamper his women to stay in their good graces.

In total, my parents had seven children: me and my six older sisters. My mother was a homemaker, so she relied heavily on my father's income. Thankfully, my two eldest sisters worked and often helped my mother pay the bills that my father neglected.

By the time I was born, my mother was at her wits' end with my father's shenanigans. He arrogantly overestimated the power of his semi-regular financial contributions and assumed my mother would never leave him. She gave him the shock of his life when she kicked him out and told him to stay with those other women because he wasn't welcome in our house anymore.

I believe my mother stayed with my father as long as she did partially because he was all she knew; in her small hometown in Mexico, he physically picked her up and carried her to his house when she was just 15 years old. She kicked and screamed but became his wife because, culturally, that was the decent thing to do. As difficult as it may be for most people to understand, she grew to love him, and he became her family. Perhaps because she didn't have family; she was orphaned as a child then taken out of school in the third grade and put to work. I've wonder what it must have felt like for her to accept the man who kidnapped her as family, have him refuse to be faithful then wind up a single mother to his children. Devastating, I presume.

She immediately picked up work doing laundry, cooking, and cleaning but the loss of my father's income hit our family hard. When I was five, my mother found a consistent job at a bed and breakfast. While this provided a steady flow of income, it simply wasn't enough. She worked around the clock and there were months where I didn't see her for more than an hour or two each day. She would often arrive home from work after midnight and awaken to go back to work at 4:00 am. I, in turn, would awaken to the smell of bleach water and the sight of our family's white dish cloths soaking in a bucket; my only indication that she had come home.

I got my first job when I was just seven years old. My friend's father owned a store, so he allowed me to sell merchandise to tourists on the beach. I worked for free but could keep any profit that I made above the selling price. Hunger motivated me to work. I can vividly recall my stomach growling while I hustled trying to make a sale. Hunger was a regular way of life for kids without fathers and kids whose parents had difficulty finding work. Sometimes I would become nauseated from not eating and throw up green stuff. I remember a little girl fainting in the first grade while standing in line. We all knew it was because she hadn't eaten.

Parents were so busy trying to provide that their kids were left to fend for themselves. Children as young as three years old would be playing in their front yard by themselves. I was taking the city bus alone when I was just six years old. On three occasions, I even saw a dead body on the street. One time, a man robbed a liquor store and was shot in the street by the store owner as he ran away. My 6-year-old self stumbled across his body on my way home.

My world was characterized by violence, abuse, and depravity. In my hood, children without fathers were subject to bullying, exploitation, and abuse. I was no exception.

Poverty was a way of life for people living in my neighborhood. The few clothes I owned had holes in them, and my shoes didn't fit; my mother would buy shoes two sizes too big so they would last 2-3 years. To preserve my shoes, I only wore them to school and would go barefoot the rest of the time. The ground would be scalding in the summer so I would run several feet then stop in the shade to let my feet cool down.

Clean water was the one thing that we had that a lot of other towns didn't perhaps because Acapulco was a hotspot for tourists. That didn't mean that I was exempt from drinking dirty water though. The small town where my father lived with his mistress didn't have a clean water source so I would walk with my half-brothers to the dirty lake to fetch drinking water. We would dig holes by the lake so the soil would act as a filter when paired against the pressure of the water's current. Due to this common practice, many of the children wound up with tapeworms and other water-related illnesses. Thankfully, we rarely visited my father because of his mistress's obvious disdain for his "wife's children" so I was spared from the regular consumption of feces-infested water.

When I was ten, my mother came down with a mysterious illness that caused spots of discoloration on her face. With no enforceable labor laws in place, her employer fired her. Extreme lack turned to *utter* destitute and despair. By this time, three of my sisters had migrated to the United States and another one had moved to Guadalajara, so it was just me, my mother and two youngest sisters living in our home. We lived solely off my income, and the money that my oldest sisters could spare.

After work, I would rush home and hand my mother everything I made. Still, all our income sources combined were only enough to provide a total of four or five eggs and some salsa for our family of four on some days. My mom would whisk the eggs for a long time to make them look large and fluffy. Throughout the day my two sisters and I would snack on those eggs instead of eating them all at once. My mom often went without so we could eat.

As I approached 13 years of age, my sisters in the US suggested that I stay with them and work. Although I'd heard stories of women getting raped and people getting shot or overheating as they migrated, life was unbearable, so I felt that I had nothing to lose. I agreed to make the trip, and that one "yes" was the *defining moment* of my life.

For my safe arrival, my two sisters agreed to pay a "coyote": a person who smuggles immigrants into the US. My neighbor and I took a two day bus ride from Acapulco to Tijuana to meet the coyote.

The coyote took us to the border of Tijuana several hours before midnight. Crowds of people stood by the gate as immigration guards watched them closely. It was like a game of cat and mouse. The coyotes knew the guards changed shifts at midnight, so we stood by a part of the fence that was torn down. People would tear down several feet of fence and US Customs and Border Protection would repair it only to have a different part of the fence be torn down. The plan was to sprint across the border when they changed guards. Midnight struck and …

"Vamos!" [Go!], yelled the coyote and we took off!

We approached a road used to patrol the area. Underneath the road was an empty water canal which we crawled through so we would not be seen. When we emerged, there was desert as far as I could see. I ran for what seemed like forever for the life I wanted. It was pitch dark with only the moonlight to guide us. Our only goal was to remain hidden within the shadows, trees, and bushes for 13.3 miles until we reached the city of Chula Vista. As we ran, a helicopter flew above us, and the coyotes told us to duck low to the ground. We were told to wear all black beforehand to remain undetected. When the helicopter retreated, we waited a decent amount of time then continued our journey. Two times, border patrol drove by in search of people crossing. When we saw the headlights of their truck, we hid and waited until it was safe to continue.

We arrived at Chula Vista around 5:00 am and continued running behind the coyote, jumping over fences, and crossing the backyards of different homes. I was terrified when I looked up and saw a man pointing a rifle at me as I sprinted across his backyard. Dogs barked and lights switched on, but we kept running until we approached a freeway and ran across.

We stopped in the shadows on the other side of the freeway, and this was the first time I was able to take it in…I was in America! The smell of pine was prominent- that smell will forever be imprinted in my mind. From there, we walked to a hidden burrow where we ate food brought to us by another coyote and slept on cardboard. The next morning, a third coyote brought a van and instructed us all to lay in a row in the back. Those were our marching orders until we arrived in LA. The coyotes timed it so we would cross the San Clemente inspection point when immigration was not there. As we passed the checkpoint, the coyotes cheered. In LA, they locked us in a house with about 20 other people and brought us roasted chicken, salsa, and tortillas. I was already eating better than I did in Mexico! They subsequently called our designated contact person, to inform them that their person had arrived and to bring the money.

***

It's been over 30 years since I stepped on American soil and I feel that I have made the most of the opportunity to live here. About a year after my arrival, I enrolled in school and joined the high school soccer team. I used to play soccer in Mexico, so I was selected to play competitive soccer in the states. I started working immediately and began sending money to my mother.

Not knowing English was difficult at first but I was determined to learn. I would spend hours translating my homework from English to Spanish before doing it. It took me about three years before I was fluent in English. Before my high school graduation, I received inquiries from Michigan State and Texas A&M but could not receive an academic or athletic scholarship because I was undocumented. Instead, I worked 50-60 hours per week to pay my college tuition. I graduated from Fresno State in 2006 and enrolled in the MS program. In 2015, I was granted residency in the US and bought a home. I currently work as a finance manager for Lithia Corp. and am eligible to apply for citizenship this year. I plan to buy an investment home later this year and can honestly say that I am living my American dream.

Transformation Tip

In life, not everyone starts on an equal playing field. We are not all born with the same resources and advantages nor do we live in a world where all things are equal. We all suffer from our own individual adversity, setbacks, and trials so it doesn't make sense to compare our progress to the progress of others. What takes one man 1 day might take another man 1 year and that's okay; the important thing is that you reach your destination- not how long it takes you to get there. For instance, when I first arrived in the US, I wanted to go to school but had to focus first on working due to my mother's circumstances in Mexico. Eventually, because I kept my eye on the target (my goal of going to school), I was able to slowly restructure my life to accommodate my enrollment in school.

Likewise, your journey is uniquely your own. So, even if you find yourself in the midst of great adversity, do not become discouraged because your progress is not like that of the next guy. Instead, stay focused on your goal and continue to persevere. You will reach your goal in your time.

Eli Sotelo *lives with his daughter, Victoria, in Clovis, CA and strives each day to be the father he never had. He is also a COVID-19 survivor. He strongly believes that, when much is given, much is expected. Through World Vision, he currently sponsors a 12-year-old boy living in India named Hemanth. Eli is proud to be Hemanth's sponsor and views his sponsorship as a way to "level the playing field" of life. His monthly contribution goes directly to Hemanth's family, as well as to community projects that enable his community to be self-sufficient. To view children in need of a sponsor, go to:*

www.teamworldvision.org/index.cfm?fuseaction=donorDrive.participant&participantID=252533

Captain of My Own Ship

By William Lurcott

In my 41 years piloting aircraft, every time I pulled back on the stick, the nose of the aircraft would rise. But not this day. When the aircraft impacted with the ocean, my indicated speed was 72 miles per hour. I could level the wings, but with the elevator jammed, I couldn't flare for a gentler impact. I remember the wheels skipped once and then dug right into the water. The aircraft instantly nosed down, the wooden propeller broke off and the windshield broke inward, allowing the waterfall to begin over the instrument panel.

Have you ever had that "falling feeling" when you're drifting off to sleep? I felt that falling feeling and that's what woke me up! The aircraft was settling from its nose down attitude back into a horizontal one. The cockpit had filled with seawater up to my chest. My first thought? I'M STILL ALIVE! But the water was rising rapidly and nearly above my shoulders. We're sinking quick here! I reached down to unbuckle my seat belt like I had done thousands of times before, but this time it wouldn't release! With the water level now above my lips, I tilted my head back to get my mouth above the seawater and took my final breath.

A quick thought entered my mind as I purposefully plunged my head below the water. Wouldn't it be ironic that a waterman (surfer, sailor, boat captain) had survived a plane crash, yet would be drowned by an unrelenting seat belt? With my head now underwater, I could see the problem. My rather long tee shirt had become entangled in the seat belt buckle. I pulled my shirt downward and the buckle was then free, and it opened easily. I swam out the aircraft's door.

When I surfaced, there were boats that I had just photographed minutes ago now just a few yards away! I swam over to them and began to toss them some belongings that I had grabbed from the sinking plane. Time seemed to have slowed down, but nothing stops gravity. In less than a minute, my little plane with its high wings now filled with water, nosed down one last time, and assumed its final dive. I felt like I was watching the Titanic go down. A part of my heart sunk watching the plane, but I was grateful to not be inside of it.

I had survived an aircraft crashing into the Atlantic Ocean, yet that turned out to be the easy part! The sudden stop, those G-forces from the crash, left my spine severely damaged. Turns out that maybe I should have gotten some X rays, MRI's or at least some medical opinions. In hindsight, that information may have revealed how damaged I was and that my back was hanging on by a thread. Sure, I knew that it was very sore, but for some reason, I didn't correlate it with real damage, just a possible bruising or something equally benign.

With my aerial photo business literally underwater, I decided to visit an out-of-town friend. We played some tennis. I made a sudden twist that normally would have been OK, but this was the final straw that broke this camel's back. I dropped to the court and couldn't get up. Pain to a degree which I had never experienced traversed through by body. I couldn't move. There was no position that I could get into that didn't have extraordinary amounts of pain.

Lying down, sitting, standing—everything and every position was excruciating. Transitioning among those postures literally took my breath away. I could barely hold myself up. The intense pain was always there, and I could not sleep because of it. I could only pass out in a state of exhaustion, and then only for a few hours at a time.

I traveled to a special Spine Clinic. They apologized for not being able to operate on this kind of injury. They said that they couldn't really fix anything. Their approach would be to drug me and ablate the nerves (kill them with some electrical current); a repetitive procedure which would only last four to six months. They made it clear that the procedure itself would not heal anything and that this would be a lifelong effort of pain management.

In the meantime, walking consisted of a slow, cautious, forward shuffle of each foot about two or three inches at a time. I couldn't spread my legs. No weight could be borne by my spine (including my own body, but I forced myself). I would use one arm to support my upper body to be able to hold weight with the other arm. For close to three years, I could not lift a gallon water jug without using the other arm to bear the weight.

I could make no sudden moves; my spine would not support them, and I would go right into a long painful series of spasms. (The MRI's revealed that I had torn my dura and was leaking cerebral spinal fluid. I had a few bulging discs and a sequestered fragment, something akin to a hangnail dangling among the nerves.) The doctors involved said they couldn't operate.

For an active person like myself, this crippling accident was like living in hell—or worse—not living at all. It seemed that I couldn't do anything that I had enjoyed in my life prior to this accident. I couldn't lift a child, hold my wife, surf, play tennis, go for a walk, ride a bike, or perform even small tasks about the home. I couldn't even make a fast move of any sort. I felt as if I could not help anyone with this body.

Climbing the 17 steps in our home always resulted in great pain and seemed to take forever. I kept hoping that things would get better, but they didn't. My relentless and tremendous pain exhibited no tendency to reduce its intensity. I felt worse than useless. I felt like a burden.

I found myself tempted to window shop self-destructive thoughts. I was faced with a reality of never again walking a normal, pain-free step in my life. Of living with constant, face-wincing, high-level pain every single day and night, forevermore. This crippling pain disallowed focused, productive work. I was physically and financially bankrupt. I took ibuprofen, but with marginal relief.

The message of the pain to me was this: Cause no further harm! Be careful regarding my movements and remember, just because I can lift or move something, doesn't mean that I should. Figuring that I would have pain regardless, there was no need to spread or share it. Because my wife is

Chapter 6: Daring Escapes

so sensitive and empathetic, I downplayed my symptoms—my limping, my muffled gasps of pain, my wincing, etc. to deny her clues. I knew if she sensed my pain, it would make her upset. Still, that much pain wore on my being, and it was exhausting on many levels.

Understandably, depression was constantly at my door, waiting for an opportunity to come into my life. But you know what? I never answered that door. Looking back on that time in my life, my wife told me that I never complained. In fact, she never knew the level of pain I was in. Because day-to-day, I still joked, I still had fun, I still brought joy to wherever I was. How did I do that?

Seldom do we have much—if any--control over the circumstances which arrive in our lives. We can only respond to the events in our lives with who and what we are at the time. I used my past to reference from, but not limit me to, what had previously worked. I looked for similarities in patterns, in experiences, and in references. I divided my current challenges into ones which were actionable from those which I could do little or nothing. Fortunately (or not) this wasn't my first rodeo.

Always it seemed to me, my pain was made worse by my resistance, by my "Not Owning" what had shown up in my world. Resisting what was there, right in front of me. Trying to act or walk normal when I really could not. Worse still, by not acknowledging or allowing whatever to bubble up from within me to my outside world. Whether withholding my voice, my gifts, or my expression, it created internal pressure. That pressure was probably what was driving this hard lesson--rather than the alternative, easier version that I could have had--were I paying more attention. *What did I need to see, to become? What do I need to say, to bring forward into this world? What was I being beckoned to become?*

I chose to remember that I always had choice. This was a *defining moment* for me. I could choose to allow this event to define me and what it meant to my life or I could choose my own definition of who I was regardless of any event. I decided that I alone would determine what all this means, that I alone would captain my ship. I knew that the specific ship that

I commanded, or the waves, or the weather or the storms were not always of my choosing or control. My control was only the set of the sails, the direction, and the course I steered by my rudder.

Call it Faith or Trust or just a knowing from having faced myriad problems. Deep in my heart, I know that behind everything is a purpose or a reason, although neither may be known to me at the time or even ever. So, if—or when—I feel confounded, I ask myself: What could this situation—this debilitation--be trying to teach me? How can I accelerate this healing? What messages are meant for me to realize or see through this event in this time? What is this experience asking for or leading me to do or to be? How can I serve even more from having this experience? What's funny or ironic about this event? How can this make me a bigger version of me?

Transformation Tip

I strive to invoke my internal observer, that higher-viewing side of me similar to the bird's-eye view that I frequently occupied. It's like getting a second opinion without ever leaving home. It's a realization that what I am experiencing is composed of two elements: the event and my interpretation of the event. I ask, what else could this mean? What else could I become from this? Who could I grow to be through this event? Despite this overwhelming pain, this seeming loss of integration in the world, a part of me knew that there were gifts in this event happening now. I ACTIVELY sought them out. I looked for them. Seek, and ye shall find. I remembered once again who I REALLY was. A soul in a body, of this body, but not the body. That allowed me to separate all this pain that I was experiencing from who I was. It didn't alleviate the pain, but the separation gave me peace in place of suffering.

William Lurcott *is the soon-to-be author of a book which reveals his program which transports individuals from their Unfamiliar, Uncharted, Unknowns successfully through to the other side- with or without a map. He is a coach, a* mastermind group leader and speaker. For more information, go to www.HigherViews.com or email William at: Lurcottstudios@Yahoo.com

Animal Karma

By Eric Stanosheck

In 2002, I lived in Alaska and was on a hunting trip with a couple of friends in the Wrangell Mountains. On day five my buddies ended up with their animals, so they were back in camp taking care of meat.

I went out on a trek alone that day going into a valley which was about seven miles from camp. This was farther back than we had ever been before. It started out as a beautiful Alaskan day but as things happen in Alaska - it changed really quickly. I was stalking in on a Dall sheep which is what I had my tag for. I was about 45 yards away from a nice Ram that could have easily been harvested.

I spent my time with the animal there and didn't pull the trigger. It was a great experience. I felt grateful that I had spent the time and allowed the animal to live.

I was hiking back to camp and knew I needed to get back before dark. In this part of Alaska, there are a lot of grizzly bears and bad things can happen to you after dark. You can get stuck against a box canyon, pinned against the waterfall or miss the trail. There are a lot of safety issues.

I started my hike back to camp and it started to snow and sleet. I put my black powder rifle up on my backpack and tied my rain tarp around it just to make sure that it wasn't getting wet. I was ascending the mountains and got to a flat plateau on top of the mountain. I noticed, about 50 yards away, there was a sow grizzly bear.

As soon as I saw her, she saw me. The situation quickly escalated into a dangerous brush with death as she immediately started charging at me low-to-the-ground. She came at me like a freight train, ears laid back, hair standing up on her neck, showing her teeth and growling. As this was happening, I heard a little squeak from about 20 yards away to my right. It was a six-month-old cub that happened to be in between us. The one thing I know is that grizzly bears are one of the most maternal animals in the world. There is nothing they won't do to protect their cubs. I was just in the wrong spot at the wrong time.

In what seemed like a split second, the distance between us went from 50 yards to 50 feet. I tried to get my gun out, but I couldn't get it untied, partially because my fingers weren't moving because I was frozen with fear. I had never experienced a situation like this before. 50 feet quickly became 20 feet and I realized there was nothing I could do except try to appear larger than life, hoping to be a little bit more intimidating.

The one thing I knew I couldn't do is flee from an apex predator, otherwise their instincts of chasing prey kick in. So, I held my ground somehow as she was coming closer. I felt terror. I felt fear. I was a ball of nerves.

Unexpectedly, she stopped abruptly about 11 feet from where I stood. I know this from afterwards when I counted it off. She slammed her feet into the ground. I stood paralyzed 11 feet away from her looking up into her eyeballs. I had grizzly bear saliva on my chest and mud on me from when she slammed her claws into the ground. Then she stood up, tilted her head, and popped her jaws. It was the sound of hitting two frying pans together as hard as you can. It rattled my bones.

At that time, as I looked up into her face, in all the terror, in the fear, I remember looking at every detail in her face thinking how beautiful this creature was. I could also smell the stench of death on her breath from eating dead animals. I feared that I was 11 feet away from my impending death.

At that point, I can't really explain how things happened, but a sense of peace came over me, just kind of a warmness in my body. So many things flashed and raced through my mind. What I took from that split-second was that I had led a blessed life. We all have our number of days and mine was up.

My instincts said I should clearly submit myself to the animal. I didn't want any suffering to happen. I didn't want to get mauled. I just wanted it to happen quickly. I turned and bowed my head to the bear and said a last prayer right there and just presented my neck hoping that she would snap it quickly and painlessly, so it would be over with.

Then everything went silent. It was quiet, with a warm sensation. I opened my eyes not even realizing I was alive. I fully expected to be watching my body and watching the bear. I thought I would be looking down onto this scene of horror as my last life experience. And that wasn't the case. My mind was scrambled, and I looked around, trying to figure out what was going on.

The sow and the cub had turned around in an instant. In the split second when I had closed my eyes, as she had come down to take her last lunge towards me, the bear had been given an opportunity to turn around and have a dignified retreat and save her cub.

As I watched her running off in the distance, about 60 yards from me at this point, I dropped my backpack, frantically ripping through it to find my video camera. As I recorded the bear, in my mind I was narrating the footage perfectly, speaking very clearly, and explaining the details of what I had just experienced. I caught footage of her as she ran up over the mountain with her cub and disappeared into the horizon.

Afterwards, I sat down and ate a granola bar from inside my backpack. It snowed and rained on me for well over an hour. A lot of things in life don't matter when you go through that.

I was getting wet and snowed on but didn't care. I spent a solid 30 minutes trying to figure out if I was alive or if my mind was just in a different place. A psychologist would probably say I had PTSD or was grasping for straws, trying to figure out if I was really still living or if this is what the afterlife felt like.

Eventually I composed myself and took the slowest hike back to camp. I truly looked at everything and marveled at the little grass growing out of the hill. I noticed the way the waterfalls trickled down the mountains. I paid attention to every single detail. Everything was so much more vivid at that point.

I got back into camp about an hour after dark and my buddies had a fire going. They were freaked out because they had hadn't heard from me. My radio didn't work in the canyon where I was, and the batteries had died. I stumbled into camp and my buddies were frantically asking questions. All I could do is tell them to look at the video. I just stared into the depths of the fire contemplating the meaning of life. What is life *truly* about? What is our purpose here? What did the situation actually mean? *Why* did it happen?

As they were watching the video, I heard a high-pitched voice, of what sounded like my daughter when she was four years old, not enunciating any words- and I came to realize that it was *my* voice on the video tape describing the scene as the bear was running away. I had thought that I was composed and narrating well but that was not the case. I was absolutely coming apart at the seams and just trying to hold onto something to give me a sense of life.

That night, I didn't sleep. We came out of field two days later and flew out with a pilot who was a biologist in the area. He had flown it many times. I recounted my story to him, and he said he could count on one hand how many people have been 11 feet away from their death with a sow grizzly bear and a cub in the mix and lived to tell that story. For three weeks after, every time I fell asleep, every time I laid down- she was there.

I could see her, hear her, smell her and it was full vivid color. It was always the same scene of that attack as if it were happening to me. One night, I finally got closure. I remember falling asleep and it was the same thing all over again. She was there but instead of me seeing it happen, I was living through the actual moment step-by-step. I saw the saliva hit my chest, I felt the mud come at me, I saw her rising up and I vividly remembered all the details. I remained sound asleep for the duration of this dream and finally slept through the night. I finally got that closure mentally.

Everything came together and I was finally able to process the fact that I was alright.

I realized that the situation happened to me for a reason.

I believe that the reason why it happened is so that I would have an opportunity to understand and share that terror only lasts for so long-but our purpose here is so much greater.

Transformation Tip

Moments in the outdoors, fluidly living with nature, provide some of the greatest adventures we can have. There are no scripts, no prediction of outcomes, everything happens as it wants to. We need to be in tune enough with our surroundings to not just survive but to also thrive. I truly feel that, if there is such thing as animal karma, then I experienced it that day as a hunter. You reap what you sew. By sparing the life of the ram, it might have saved my own life.

I also realized how powerful faith and prayer are when I was out there in the wild. It is so important to be knowledgeable on predators when you are out in the wilderness. Being aware of bear instincts and submissive at the same time, made the bear feel less threatened and allowed her a dignified retreat. There was no other communication or time for explanation, bargaining, strategy, etc.

I think being grateful and finding the beauty in every circumstance, even in the face of death, might have shifted the energy in that space to alter the potential outcome.

My advice to outdoor enthusiasts is this: be adventurous, explore our natural world, be aware and in tune with nature.

Eric Stanosheck lives in Haslet, Texas with his wife and four children. He is an avid outdoorsman and can be regularly found fishing or hunting anywhere he can. His email tagline reads "Life without adventure is no life at all" and he lives that to the fullest in the outdoors each year. Professionally, he is a Regional Manager for Best Version Media and creates custom furniture and lighting fixtures out of naturally cast deer and elk antlers that he and his father pick up annually (www.AntlerPicasso.com). He can be reached via email at: Eric@AntlerPicasso.com

---

Chowchilla Children: Kidnapped, Buried Alive and Survived...
By Lynda Carrejo Labendeira

Summer School

Flashback to summer July 15, 1976. It was our nation's bicentennial and the next to the last day of summer school. There was no place on Earth that I'd rather have been than summer school. We, the big kids, fourth grade and up got to go swimming three days a week. This was quite the privilege compared to the little kids who only got to swim at the Chowchilla town pool on Tuesdays and Thursdays. Yes, it was school, but way more fun because it was summer school held at Dairyland Elementary.

I loved summer school because the teachers made learning fun. The morning routines included our usual reading, writing, and math but it was the afternoon electives for arts, crafts, music, sewing, woodwork, ceramics, and games that made summer school really special. The teachers shared friendly, magnetic smiles causing us students to want to run over and give them a huge hug, especially Miss Kirk.

Chapter 6: Daring Escapes

That year I got to have Mr. Gwartney for my 4th grade summer school teacher. He was so handsome that all the 4th grade girls had crushes on him. You know, the kind of crush that makes you want to listen, learn, and do your best. Students always want to do their best for the nice teachers.

Summer school was more than worth getting up at 6:00 am to wash my face, eat a bowl of Cheerios with sliced bananas, comb my long, wavy, dark brown hair, brush my teeth then race all the way to the Wilson Jr. High School Bus Stop to catch the 7 a.m. school bus.

We had been preparing bicentennial plays, songs, and other fun, patriotic activities for weeks. The morning was filled with our usual reading, writing, and math lessons, whereas this particular afternoon we got to play water games in stations like slip and slide, water balloon tosses, and bubble gum blowing contests.

I'm pretty sure that it was Mr. Gwartney who played the fun, popular music on his record player, while we enjoyed popsicles on a thrilling Thursday afternoon.

When school was over, we loaded up onto our respective buses. My sisters and I rode bus #1 with our bus driver, Edward Ray.

The White Van

On our bus ride home from school, we typically sang the latest hits from the radio. In the middle of a country road, I spotted ahead a white Chevy van with its hood propped up.

"That's odd... a white van with its hood propped up...maybe they broke down," I thought to myself.

"My mama told me, you better shop around," we continued singing.

Edward had to slow the bus down to a complete stop in order to make his way around the parked van to ask these people if they needed help. Suddenly, three masked men with pantyhose over their faces and long rifles ordered Edward to get to the back of the bus. Edward followed their directions with my frightened 12-year-old sister, Irene, following behind him.

"We didn't do it! We didn't do it!" Jeff Brown jokingly shouted while waving his arms up in the air. Jeff was known as our class comedian, so he dealt with this intense situation the only way he knew how.

I saw the big guns and immediately sensed danger, so I quickly ducked under my seat.

One of the guys took over driving the bus. Another guy pointed his long rifle at us, telling us to be quiet and no one would get hurt. Subsequently, a third guy drove that white Chevy van while following as a guard closely behind us.

As they drove us towards the big dip of the Berenda Slough, I saw DJ and Lisa Barletta's house out in the distance. Some guy was out on the golden wheat field driving a big John Deere tractor. We were too far away for him to see what was actually going on with the bus.

Turn! Bump! Jolt! The kidnapper drove our bus down into The Berenda Slough or canal with bamboo about 25 feet high and as high up as the road.

"Ouch!" yelled a child.

"I want my mommy!" cried another younger girl.

"I want my daddy!" demanded a younger boy.

"Where are you taking us?" questioned a big kid.

"Aaaaaaaah!" I screamed.

"Waaaaah!" cried a little child.

"Shut up!" yelled a kidnapper.

Immediately, the bus went silent. We were all too scared to make a sound.

Parked in the brush was a dark green van, much like the white Chevy van. The bus finally came to a halt. The kidnapper who drove the school bus opened up the door. Then, the white van was backed up to the bus door.

"Half of you will go into this van," ordered the guy with the big rifle.

The front half of the bus, which was mostly boys along with Lisa Barletta in the seat ahead of me, despondently walked into the white van. I had a split second to decide if I should sit up and follow along like a good girl or remain hidden under my seat. They have guns, so I had better follow along and not cause any trouble. I tearfully left my sisters who were sitting more towards the back of the bus.

The kidnappers closed the back door to the white van behind me, then began to drive us away. Some hours later, I began to cry.

"Don't worry, we'll be ok." my boyfriend, Jeff Brown, assured me.

"It's not that. I have to pee so bad that it hurts. I have been holding it all day." I shared in painful embarrassment.

Jeff waited a moment, then gently took my hand and placed it upon his wet, blue jean pants. "See it's ok."

I continued to hold it.

A while later, the van stopped. It sounded as though we were at a gas station.

"Please, sirs, we are hungry! We want our mommies! We want our daddies!" the children petitioned in the dark.

"Shut up in there!" scolded the kidnapper.

"Please sirs, we need to use the restroom!" I pleaded.

"I said to shut up!" the kidnapper scolded as he pounded on the side of the van.

The Hole

We continued riding along in the dark as cargo in the back of a shipping van not knowing where nor why the kidnappers took us.

Finally, we stopped. One of the kidnappers opened up the door and told us to come out one at a time. I didn't know what to do. I didn't want to be first nor the last one out of the van. Mike Marshall went first; he was the biggest kid and happened to be a cowboy. He was followed by Lisa Barletta, then my cousin, Robert Gonzalez, and Jeff Brown.

"I may as well get it over with," I thought as I followed.

"Oh no!" Edward was in his Fruit of the Loom Underwear.

"This is a very scary and serious situation!" I thought to myself... poor Edward, how embarrassing to be forced down to your underwear. I had never seen a boy in his underwear in my entire life so the sight of a grown man made me uncomfortable.

Edward smiled assuredly so that I would not be too scared.

I began to cry profusely.

"You'll be ok," one of the kidnappers stated.

"Are you kidding me? You are pointing rifles at us and have taken us from our mommies and daddies, school, and homes," I thought to myself.

"What is your name?" asked another one of the kidnappers.

I had a split second decision to make. Should I tell them my real name or a fake name? They probably already know because of my sisters...

"Lynda," I whimpered.

"What is your last name?"

"Carrejo," I cried.

"What is your address?"

"....Alameda," more tears.

"Phone number?"

"665-2028," I reported with hesitance.

"Ok, give me your purse. And go down those stairs," commanded the kidnapper.

"Poor Edward!" I thought while climbing down the steps of the ladder towards several piles of mattresses. I began to cry some more, confused and overwhelmed with all that had been going on. As I descended into The Hole and onto the mattresses, I took a panoramic view of what would become our underground tomb...a burial chamber of sorts. There were six piles of mattresses- three rows long and two columns across.

How long are they planning to keep us here? I wondered with apprehensive bewilderment.

I caught a glimpse of my three sisters: Irene, Julia, and Stella along with the other children who I later found out were forced into the green van.

"They're alive!" I thought feeling somewhat relieved.

After clambering my way across the lumpy mattresses, I hugged my sisters and several of the other children. Then I made my way over towards a plywood area where there were some boxes of cereal, bread, peanut butter, and water. I noticed that the children were ravaging the food, so I hid a few items in between two piles of mattresses.

The kidnappers continued questioning until all of the children were sent down The Hole.

The smashed up, stocking faced abductors finally ordered Edward to get down into The Hole. They told him to keep us quiet and that they would be back. The kidnappers sealed off the top of The Hole with a metal plate. I heard digging and shoveling. The only tool left behind was the flashlight that Edward had used to guide us down into The Hole.

"Sirs, where are you going?" asked one of the children.

"When will you be back?" asked another.

"We want our Mommies!" cried a boy.

"We want our Daddies!" pleaded a girl.

"Silence!" charged the kidnapper.

The little children cried for mommies and daddies. The older children held and tried to comfort the younger ones.

"We should try to get some rest," said Edward.

"We should sing," I urged my sisters.

"He's Got the Whole World in His Hands," we sang.

Next Song, "If You're Happy and You Know It Clap Your Hands". Nobody clapped.

Suddenly, a big boom sounded with dirt falling everywhere. A big beam that was holding up the ceiling was kicked over by my hyperactive cousin, Andres.

"Aaaaaah!" screamed my sister Julia.

"Stop it!" shouted one of the girls.

"Settle down!" yelled one of the boys.

"Everyone settle down and try to get some rest." suggested Edward.

The beam was bumped again because Andres had such a hard time sitting in one place for long periods of time.

"Edward, you have to get us out of here! The place is going to cave in." we begged.

"Please, Edward, you have to get us out of here!" we urged.

Reluctantly, Edward attempted to budge the metal plate, but no luck. Quite honestly, it's hard to imagine the immense pressure of being the only adult in charge of the health and safety of twenty-six children.

"Edward, try again!" begged one of the children.

"Please, Edward!" pleaded another.

Edward tried again to no avail.

Andres bumped the 2 by 4 post once again.

We begged Edward to please try again, but realized he was not gonna risk it.

So, we began to beg Mike Marshall.

Mike thoughtfully climbed over towards the metal plate that sealed us in. He stretched his arms and legs with all his might and barely budged the metal plate. It quickly fell right back into place, but we saw it move and that gave us hope.

"It moved! I saw it move! Try it again, Mike!" I shouted.

"It's our only way out, Mike!" encouraged Jeff.

"You can do it, Mike!" Julia cheered.

"Edward, please help him. We will die here. We have got to get out! They aren't out there. They aren't coming back! They would have said something by now," we begged.

Edward finally agreed. The big kids and Edward piled up several mattresses from each of the other stacks in order to build as high a foundation as possible for the upward dig.

Edward, Mike, Jeff and Robert began digging with their bare fingers pushing the dirt up and out, up and out, up and out. The only make-shift tool was the flashlight. Edward and Mike slowly budged the metal plate that sealed us in. As they dug, dirt fell on top of them, into their eyes, into the van, and onto the mattresses.

While the guys dug, I was super scared that the kidnappers would come and shoot us for having tried to escape. I hid between the shorter stack of mattresses and the built-in plywood toilets then began praying...

"Dear God, please protect Edward and the boys digging. Please don't let those bad guys come back. Please, please, please let us all get out alive.

Please help us all get back to our mommies and daddies. I promise to be the best girl ever for the rest of my life."

After hours and hours of digging, Edward walked over for some water. He had cut his hands and his forehead. I offered to wipe his forehead clean. He allowed me. Then he walked back over for more digging until the plate was completely uncovered and the giant trucker batteries, which were placed on top of the plate to seal us in for added pressure, were moved.

In total, the boys and Edward defied the weight of a metal plate, at least six huge trucker batteries and roughly six feet of dirt with their bare hands- all intended to seal us into The Hole which we later learned was a moving van. They dug, and dug, and dug through their exhaustion. They were on a mission to escape.

They did it! They opened up The Hole.

One at a time, Edward and the boys began to lift children out of The Hole. When the last child was lifted out, we cautiously walked around a lengthy row of bushes to a machine shop of some sort.

Edward walked toward a man who was up high on a stairwell. It looked like an office.

Immediately, the man knew who we were.

"I know who you are. The Whole World has been looking for you. The world has been looking for all of you," he announced.

The man immediately called the police. Police cars and a bus labeled Santa Rita Rehabilitation Center (SRRC) picked us up and took us to the SRRC for medical care, food, police questioning and FBI interrogation. There were also news reporters with big cameras. I didn't really understand what was happening. All I knew was that I was relieved to be out of The Hole.

From the Santa Rita Rehabilitation Center, we were escorted to Chowchilla by way of a chartered Greyhound bus on Hwy 99. We drove past Los Banos where there was an exchange between the Alameda County

Police escorts and the Madera County California Highway Patrol and Sheriffs' Department.

It was an awfully long way to Chowchilla, but once we saw the Palm Trees along Robertson Boulevard, we knew that we were home.

Transformation Tip

What have I learned despite the fact that I was kidnapped and buried alive? I learned to appreciate each moment in life, to live life to the fullest and to try things fearlessly yet cautiously. I learned the importance of perseverance; without it we would have never emerged from The Hole. I learned the meaning of powerful prayer with God and how to keep my promise to be the best person that I could possibly be in my little world. I learned to appreciate the importance of each person- no matter who they are- young or old, rich or poor. Every life matters. Smile, Pray, Sing, Dance, Love and Persevere with all your heart.

Lynda Carrejo Labendeira *is a small-town girl born and raised in Chowchilla, California. At the young age of 10, she survived the world-infamous kidnapping and live burial of 26 school aged children (ages 4 to 14) along with their bus driver, Edward Ray. She is currently an elementary school teacher in Fresno, California,-and will be releasing her autobiography entitled, "Chowchilla Children: Kidnapped, Buried Alive & Beyond". To inquire about pre-ordering her book, email Lynda at ChowchillaChildren1976@gmail.com.*

Fleeing Iran For Freedom
By Soodabeh Mokry, RN, CHt

My *defining moment* occurred during my first term at nursing school when I was just 19 years old. We heard the government was planning to close all the universities and colleges in the country. Students or teachers who did not believe in the Iran government's religious ideology would not be allowed back in when the school reopened – if they were reopened. It seemed as though Iran were moving backward, even that it might entirely reject its history as one of the most educated countries on the planet. But it wouldn't close our schools indefinitely without a fight from us. A nationwide protest was scheduled: on the same day, all students, and teachers, all over Iran would protest. Hameed had persuaded me to join the movement.

"I will join the protest here right after taking my mid – term exam," I told my husband, Hameed, the day before the protest.

The next day, I lounged on the stairs of the university's front entrance, talking with my friends. We were still teenagers – it felt like nothing to our youthful systems to socialize, take a test, and protest, all in one day. Suddenly, we heard gun – shots; one after another, followed by screaming. Every-one was terrified, running to find a safe place to hide, not knowing what had happened. My friends and I found ourselves in the courtyard, but we were not safe there. We were quickly mobbed, surrounded by violent, angry men and women with guns, baseball bats, knives, and rocks. They hit us on the heads, arms, legs, everywhere.

Then, I felt a strong hand pushed me from the back, and I fell onto the cement. They continued beating me. I gasped for air as others fell on top of me. Then the weight started to be lifted; the people on top of me were being dragged away- I heard their screams for their captors to release them. And then I was lifted roughly from the ground. They threw us in a truck, pointing their big guns at us, screaming profanities. I was frightened, thinking about my mom, who had no idea where I was. *What will she do if I die? And Hameed- what is happening to him?* I thought.

It was a hot summer day; we were all soaked with sweat and getting hotter by the second because we were crammed together; with no room to move at all. Everyone was quiet, afraid to say anything. I could hear my heart beating extremely fast in my chest, feel my head pounding and throbbing from the pain. I couldn't stop thinking about air and how there seemed to be none. There was no space between us; it seemed as if we were one big pile of flesh.

The truck stopped, and I heard the sound of a large metal door opening. Then the truck's door opened and all we could see were guns pointed at us, and there was shouting for us to get out of the truck. We entered a yard more than ten feet long and surrounded by tall dark- brown- and- red brick walls. There were several male guards, dressed in green army uniforms, with short dark hair and thick black beards, their faces red and eyes bulging, shouting, "Go, go, go! Move, move!" They led us into a dark room about the size of a basketball court. There was one small window, with vertical black metal bars, very high near the ceiling. We couldn't see anything outside the window, and no one outside could see what was going on inside that room.

Without air-conditioning or a fan, the room quickly filled with the foul odor of sweat mixed with vomit and urine. I wanted to throw up. One of the guards shoved me, and I fell. I got up and tucked myself into a far corner. I looked around the room, at the many other bloodied or bowed faces. I was filled with terror; my body shook uncontrollably, and tears streamed down my face.

My head felt like it was about to explode as the sharp pain at the back of my skull grew. I started hyperventilating. Subsequently, I felt the room spinning, and my eyes blurred. I could hear ringing in my ears as I slumped to the floor unconscious.

I woke up one week later in the hospital with special prison guards outside of my room. The prison staff had taken me to the hospital and had planned to transport me back to prison once I was well.

I was frightened and didn't know what had happened to me or my classmates. With the grace of God and the help of my mother's cousin who was a director of nursing in the state, I was able to be released from the hospital so I didn't have to go back to prison.

I had no idea why I had survived. I had nightmares about it every single night.

Eventually I moved past this horrific nightmare and Hameed and I married in 1981. After we wed, we decided to start a family, so I was no longer active on the political scene. Hameed continued to organize political activities underground.

Due to the increased danger in what he was doing, he kept his political activities a secret from me so I wouldn't know anything in case he was ever captured. His work was making ripples and inciting people to press for change. One of the activists in his group got caught and he was savagely tortured and eventually leaked the names of everyone in their political activist group.

Hameed and I both knew that he would be killed if he stayed in Iran. His family gave him money to escape to the United States and I sold all our belongings and used the money to stay behind. He promised that he would send for me as soon as he settled.

Three years went by and he still had not sent for me. My family kept telling me that he was gone and wasn't going to bring me to the US. They even speculated that he had met someone else.

In a last-ditch effort to reunite me with my husband, my brother arranged to take me to Turkey to visit the American Embassy. Unfortunately, he died in a tragic car accident and I never made it to the Embassy. When Hameed heard of my brother's passing, he arranged for me to go to Turkey to stay with his friends so they could help me get my paperwork in order to come to America. Eventually, we got all our ducks in a row and I immigrated to the United States with our 6-year-old son and 2-year-old daughter.

However, when I got to the US, things between Hameed and I were not as they used to be. I was devastated and heartbroken. I had waited three years to be reunited with Hameed, my husband of ten years. I had sacrificed my safety, my job, and my family to join him in our new home in the United States. Now, it felt like I had wasted, rather than given, so much time, energy, and money to be here, to be happy, to be free.

Chapter 6: Daring Escapes

I was living with a man whom I no longer knew and, perhaps even worse, who no longer seemed to recognize me.

I felt hopeless and frightened, but I knew I had to confront him. I had to know the answer. I had never been good at confronting others. My body reacted in that old way, shaking, my heart thudding. But I felt strong, rooted in those words. I had the truth on my side. He would have been killed in Iran, had I not made his leaving possible by staying behind and working and raising our children, all within the toxic space of my family home.

"Hameed, I don't know what is wrong with you, but I can't stand it anymore. You need to tell me what is happening, please. After everything I did for our family and saving your life by letting you escape Iran, you owe me that much."

Hameed looked at me, finally. I could see his eyes were red, and his face had become pale, as if the blood had left his veins. He was surprised that I had demanded an answer. I took strength from that too.

"I didn't want to tell you this, but you keep pushing me. I love and care for you, but I am not in love with you anymore. I have been thinking about this for a long time. I am not crazy; I don't want to give you a false hope, thinking we are together. I hope you understand." He spoke firmly, but gently.

I knew he was talking, but I couldn't hear anything. I felt frozen, yet dizzy, yet unable to feel my body from head to toe. Shortly after, I realized I could move. I got up, walked into the living room, and lay down on the cold floor. I felt my heart stop beating, yet I could still see Hameed, sitting there.

Hameed stood up and sighed in my direction before leaving the apartment.

I pressed my palms against the floor. I hadn't had high expectations, just to have a roof over my head, a small room I could call my own, and to live happily with the man I had loved for many years - my husband - and the father of my children. But I realized, suddenly, sharply, that it had been a luxury to wish for that alone. Because without Hameed, this place was yet another prison.

I had no other family or friends here. I did not have money or a way of earning it. I could not speak the language. I thought the deaths of my father and then my brother were the worst heartaches I would experience, but I was wrong.

The thought of living with Hameed knowing he didn't love me was unbearable. The thought of living without him, seemed impossible. *Oh, dear God, who is going to take care of me now?*

I knew going back to Iran was completely out of the question. I had severed those ties. Besides, I couldn't bear to hurt my children. They deserved to be with their father.

I felt the odds were against me. I felt I was doomed to suffer for the rest of my life. So, I decided to end my life, but failed miserably.

Feeling defeated, I decided to let Hameed go and try to move on with my life. My faith in God and the love I had for my children helped me to move forward. I woke up every day reminding myself to breathe, to take a shower, to walk a few more steps, to go outside, to talk to people even thought I didn't know the language.

I dreamed of going back to school and becoming a nurse. I was a nurse in Iran and passionate about helping people to overcome health challenges. However, I had to go back to school to obtain a degree in nursing to work in America.

One day when Hameed came to pick up the kids, I told him about my dream.

"I am going to go to school and get my nursing degree," I said with excitement like a little, innocent girl.

He started laughing. "Are you serious? Do you know how difficult it is? You can't even speak English yet."

"Why, do you think it's difficult? I am going to work hard and start the program when I am ready. I am going to be able to work as a nurse!" I replied firmly standing up with my hands on my hips filled with confidence, looking directly into his eyes. "I will show you, Hameed. Trust me, I will make it without you, I promise!"

"Listen, Soodabeh. The closest you can come to working in a hospital is to clean the toilets," he continued laughing, and then he left.

I had been listening to Hameed for many years keep telling me I couldn't make decisions, or I wasn't able to take care of myself without the help of others. I lived every day believing I would literally die without him. I realized his statement about me being incapable of choosing and doing what I wanted was the fire I needed in my gut to keep going and prove him wrong. I had heard such comments from him and his sister before, but at that moment, I finally decided to refuse to believe them. This was also a *defining moment* for me.

I felt life had given me another chance. I felt I was born again. I had dreams and aspirations. I was alive. I realized listening to others who didn't do anything to help me was just wasting my time. I was determined to make it and create the most beautiful life possible for me in America. I wasn't afraid of working hard. I had worked fifteen days in a row over and over when I was in Iran as a nurse.

I had raised my children while working and without any emotional or physical support from my family for three years. I began thinking and believing I was able to make decisions. I decided that day that I would succeed no matter what. I realized I made the perfect decision to let Hameed leave. It was a new time, a new beginning. I was proud and ready to start making new decisions for my family alone.

And, I was able to succeed. In three years, I learned to speak the language, go to school, and graduate as a registered nurse. Overcoming life challenges, I found my passion and life purpose, to help others to do the same. That was the reason I wrote my first book, *Angel Nightingale* four years ago.

Sharing my story, I want to inspire you to believe in miracles – miracles created by you when you set boundaries, quit with the excuses, shame, guilt, and blame, and use the power you already have to be better, do better, and find peace within.

Believe me when I say that you have more than what I had twenty - nine years ago. You can speak the language. You know where to go, who to talk to for help. We live in the internet age. You can search for and find every answer.

But ultimately, though you should seek help, the answer is not outside you. Just as you are the only one who can break you, you are the only one who can help you. You are the only one who can rescue you and love you unconditionally.

I grew up feeling I never belonged. I was different from all my family. I was told by many family members, friends, and even co-workers that I wasn't enough because I was short. I was told I wasn't allowed to decide, so I was unable to make any decision for myself. I was weak in the face of my family's high expectations, so I had no self-esteem or confidence of any sort. I was no one without my family, and I was no one without my husband.

What crossroads are you standing at?

What's a truly terrifying situation you experienced?

Are you feeling alone, scared, isolated, and hopeless?

Are you stressed, overwhelmed, or confused about your future?

If you are feeling hopeless, if you feel you have no choice, think again. The possibilities are endless when you decide to live, to love, to forgive, to take responsibility, and to be accountable for creating the life you want and deserve.

No matter what your situation is, facing life challenges, you have the power to choose and decide to change your circumstance. Let go of that unhealthy situation and move forward.

Because the payouts are massive. If you live ready and accepting of all the changes coming to you, life becomes interesting, surprising, and magical.

If you need support or information on resources in this book, please email: Melanie@MyDefiningMoments.com or visit our website: www.MyDefiningMoments.com

If you would like to join our free book club and interact with authors of your favorite books, please visit here: https://www.definingmoments.kartra.com/page/l9c189

Thank you for reading our book. We appreciate an honest review here:

https://www.amazon.com/dp/B08GC1FLPB

Transformation Tip

Start today by choosing *you*. Accept your situation and decide what you want. What are you passionate about? What are your dreams and your heart's desires? Take action steps to achieve your goals.

If you don't know what to do or how to achieve your goals, then invest in yourself by talking to an expert or finding a mentor. You are significant. You matter. You are precious, you are worthy, you are perfect. You have the power to create your destiny.

I am here to help you. I am here to cheer you on. Choose today. Decide you deserve to be happy, healthy, and fulfilled. It's never too late to start your life over. The choice is yours.

Soodabeh Mokry, *the author of Angel Nightingale, is a motivational speaker, certified hypnotherapist, Holistic wellness, and alternative health coach. Supported by her thirty years of medical experience and the data behind both Western and alternative wellness techniques, Soodabeh empowers people by providing the step-by-step tools to achieve their goals.*

Soodabeh has worked with people suffering with heart disease, diabetes, cancer, depression, anxiety, and chronic pain – many of whom come to her after other attempts and relapses. Soodabeh believes that there is always hope, and she is committed to helping people live healthy and happy lives. To contact Soodabeh, go to www.soodabehmokry.com or email her at info@soodabehmokry.com.

You can find her book, Angel Nightingale, here: https://amzn.to/33fgrka

Conclusion

Grab Hold of the Ring Buoy

In life, no one is exempt from suffering. We ALL suffer at one point or another. We all face individual hardships and deal with them in a way that is unique to who we are as individuals (our experiences, value system, personality etc.)

Sometimes life knocks the wind out of us, and we find ourselves hunched over gasping for breath or in a fetal position feeling helpless, hopeless, and fearful of the future.

In these situations—when your world is crashing down- it's important to remember that you have the ability to tap into and draw strength from a higher power. You were not created to go through life as a victim, weak, helpless, or inconsolable. You are too pleasantly complex and endowed with purpose, gifts, and talents to stay in a place of defeat.

So, what does defeat look like? Defeat looks like hopelessness. It's when we surrender to the idea that there is nothing great for us in the future. The truth is that none of us can know exactly what the future holds. Since the future is unknown, a mystery in many ways, we can only speculate what we think is likely to happen. And why make predictions from a place of frustration, discouragement, and distress when a negative emotional state inclines you to make predictions that do not serve you? Instead, we must be intentional about the thoughts that we entertain and the emotions that we give ourselves over to.

We MUST choose to have hope…in ALL circumstances.

Charles Darwin eloquently expressed mankind's need for hope when he stated the following, *"Man can live about forty days without food, about three days without water, about eight minutes without air, but only for one second without hope."*

Survivors do not bow down to hopelessness. Instead they recognize hope as the lifeline that they so desperately need. They grasp for it and cling to it like a drowning person grasps and clings to a lifeguard's ring buoy. And once they grab hold of it, they don't let it go!

A survivor *will* fight the storms of life in search of a better life. They continually remind themselves that better days are ahead. That even in the darkest times, there is always something to be grateful for.

Having hope is an act of faith and an act of courage, therefore, it's heroic. Too often people resist hopefulness because they don't want to be disappointed but, ironically, living without hope is awfully disappointing. It is like deciding to build your home in a pit of despair- why would you want to live in those conditions?!

You are not destined to LIVE in any negative emotion. NOT pain, anger, frustration or unforgiveness. These emotions are meant to be passed through like passageways leading you to a more evolved version of yourself. The length of time that it takes to get "through" will vary depending on the circumstance and level of pain associated with the circumstance. However, steps should be taken so that the negative emotions do not become the permanent default state of your heart.

When painful experiences happen to us, we are to work through residual trauma and tough emotions so that we can rid ourselves of unresolved issues, triggers, and errors in thinking while still RETAINING the lessons from those experiences. Oh yes, there is something to be learned from every experience. There is no such thing as failure, if growth occurred. We just have to be humble and teachable enough to extract the wisdom.

And sometimes, we will never understand why something happened to us. Not while we are living on this earth anyway. In times like these it is ever so important to be mindful of what you focus on. Instead of continually replaying the incident over and over again in your mind in an attempt to figure out *why* it happened, focus on being grateful for the lesson and hopeful for the future. While we can speculate why something happened, the truth is that we can never know for sure. We run the risk of staying stuck in the past when we refuse to accept that we may never know the reason why something happened.

Humans are resilient. The stories in this book are proof that we have the capacity to overcome the harshest of circumstances.

I believe the common theme in all of the stories in this book is the author's refusal to be a victim. Even when circumstances happened *to* them, they refused to surrender their power by believing that their response to the circumstances had no effect on the situation. Instead, they placed the power to change their life in their own hands by taking ownership of its current condition. Then they took strategic action to manifest the life they envisioned. In essence, they became survivors by refusing to be victims. I believe this is key to transforming your life.

> *"The victim mindset dilutes the human potential. By not accepting personal responsibility for our circumstances, we greatly reduce our power to change them."*
>
> **— Steve Maraboli**

There is a survivor inside ALL of us. WE ARE POWERFUL. Never accept the lie that you are not in control of your own life. You are. You have the power to choose. Grab hold of the ring buoy...

You are a survivor. You are never truly alone in that quest.

Acknowledgements

Thank you to my co-author, Amber Torres, for dedicated nearly a year to finding, editing, and even writing so many of the stories in this book. Your dedication to detail and tone has made all the difference in this book.

Thanks to my Mom, Judy Warner, for serving as an additional editor. You have always been up to the task and have been reading my work for over four decades now.

Thank you to all of the contributing authors. Your stories of courage have inspired me. It's an honor to include so many valuable life lessons in this book.

— Melanie Warner

Thank you to my mentor, Melanie Warner, for taking me under your wing and showing me the ropes of publishing my first book! Your wisdom, guidance and encouragement have been a Godsend.

To all the authors that contributed a story in this book. It was an honor to be able to work closely with you and hear what your experiences taught you. You are all examples of what it means to be a survivor.

To Eli Sotelo for always supporting my work and helping me take care of the littles. You're the MVP of co-parents

To Pastor Lisa, for always believing that there is greatness inside of me and for always encouraging me to walk in destiny, identity, and victory.

To my best friend and Pastor, Frances Almaguer, thank you for being my treasured friend and confidant. My closest of kin. Thank you for caring as much about my spiritual walk and personal growth as you care about me – your old pal, Ambi.

— Amber Torres

About the Authors

Melanie Warner is a #1 bestselling author, speaker, publisher, and entrepreneur. She is the founder of the *Defining Moments* book series that offer positive stories of hope and healing from people who have overcome extreme challenges in life.

Warner was a successful magazine publisher for over 20 years and then tragedy hit her family when her son died. That emotional shut down led to divorce, shutting down her company, then bankruptcy, foreclosure and even tax court. What had taken her 20 years to build was gone over night. She had to rebuild her entire life from scratch - and found a way to do it in only two years.

This experience inspired her to write the first book of the series - *Defining Moments: Coping With the Loss of a Child* (https://www.amazon.com/dp/B07X2FGPCJ) as a resource for bereaved families. Her book hit the bestseller list in only 2 weeks.

After that, she was inundated with requests to help others get their book completed, published and marketed. She teaches people how to write a book that is profitable and how to align it with a business that makes a difference for others.

Melanie is also a book coach who helps people write, publish and launch their own books. Do you want to share your story with the world? Apply to work with us online @ www.MyDefiningMoments.com or email Melanie@MyDefiningMoments.com

 **Amber Torres** earned a bachelor's degree in business management and a certificate in marketing from CSU Fresno, in 2011. After graduation, she launched an at-home, business writing company providing human resource and marketing material. Amber's passion in life is to use her gift of writing to acquire funds for initiatives that create positive and sustainable social impact at home and abroad. The global water crisis is one such initiative.

She is the mother of two children and a volunteer child ambassador for World Vision; a Christian Humanitarian organization that works to address the root causes of poverty and injustice (www.worldvision.org).

To sponsor a child through World Vision, visit:

https://www.worldvision.org/sponsor-a-child/

About Defining Moments Press

Built for aspiring authors who are looking to share transformative ideas with others throughout the world, Defining Moments Press offers life coaches, healers, business professionals, and other non-fiction or self-help authors a comprehensive solution to get their book published without breaking the bank or taking years.

Defining Moments Press prides itself on bringing readers and authors together to find tools and solutions for everyday problems.

As an alternative to self-publishing or signing with a major publishing house - we offer full profits to our authors, low-priced author copies, and simple contract terms.

Most authors get stuck trying to navigate the technical end of publishing. The comprehensive publishing services offered by Defining Moments Press mean that your book will be designed by an experienced graphic artist, available in printed, hard copy format, and coded for all eBook readers, including the Kindle, iPad, Nook, and more.

We handle all of the technical aspects of your book creation so you can spend more time focusing on your business that makes a difference for other people.

Defining Moments Press founder, publisher and #1 bestselling author, Melanie Warner, has over 20 years of experience as a writer, publisher, master life coach and accomplished entrepreneur.

You can learn more about Warner's innovative approach to self-publishing or take advantage of free trainings and education at: MyDefiningMoments.com

Defining Moments Book Publishing

If you're like many authors, you have wanted to write a book for a long time, maybe you have even started a book... but somehow, as hard as you have tried to make your book a priority - other things keep getting in the way.

Some authors have fears about their ability to write or whether or not anyone will value what they write or buy their book. For others, the challenge is making the time to write their book or having accountability to finish it.

It's not just finding the time and confidence to write that is an obstacle. Most authors get overwhelmed with the logistics of finding an editor, finding a support team, hiring an experienced designer, and figuring out all the technicalities of writing, publishing, marketing, and launching a book. Others have actually written a book and might have even published it but did not find a way to make it profitable.

For more information on how to participate in our next Defining Moments Author Training program visit: www.MyDefiningMoments.com. Or you can email melanie@MyDefiningMoments.com

Other #1 Best Selling Books by Defining Moments™ Press

- *Defining Moments: Coping With the Loss of a Child* - by Melanie Warner
- *Write your Bestselling Book in 8 Weeks or Less and Make a Profit - Even if No One Has Ever Heard of You* - by Melanie Warner
- *Become Brilliant: Roadmap From Fear to Courage* – by Shiran Cohen
- *Rise, Fight, Love, Repeat: Ignite Your Morning Fire* - by Jeff Wickersham
- *Life Mapping: Decoding the Blueprint of Your Soul* - by Karen Loenser
- *Ravens and Rainbows: A Mother-Daughter Story of Grit, Courage and Love After Death* – by L. Grey and Vanessa Lynn
- *Pivot You! 6 Powerful Steps to Thriving During Uncertain Times* – by Suzanne R. Sibilla
- *A Workforce Inspired: Tools to Manage Negativity and Support a Toxic-Free Workplace* – by Dolores Neira.
- *Focus on Jesus and Not the Storm: God's Non-Negotiable to Christians in America* - by Keith Kelley
- *Emerging You: a New Path to Leaving the Past Behind, Finding Your Purpose, and Becoming the Best Version of You* - by Soodabeh Mokry
- *7 Unstoppable Starting Powers: Powerful Strategies for Unparalleled Results From Your First Year as a New Leader* - by Olusegun Eleboda
- *Friendship Choices: 5 Great Lessons on Choosing the Right Friends* - by Benedictta Apraku
- *Stepping Out, Moving Forward: Songs and Devotions* - by Jacqueline O'Neil Kelley